BECOMING Legend

BECOMING Legend

The Billion-Dollar Blueprint to Be a Whale in a Sea of Sharks

BERNER

HARMONY
NEW YORK

Harmony Books
An imprint of Random House
A division of Penguin Random House LLC
1745 Broadway, New York, NY 10019
harmonybooks.com | randomhousebooks.com
penguinrandomhouse.com

Illustrations by Jeremy Fish

ISBN 978-0-593-73664-7
Ebook ISBN 978-0-593-73665-4

Printed in the United States of America

1st Printing

FIRST EDITION

BOOK TEAM: Production editor: Luke Epplin • Managing editor: Allison Fox • Production manager: Katie Zilberman • Copy editor: Martin Schneider • Proofreaders: Michael Burke, Kevin Clift, Kathryn Jones

Book design by Ralph Fowler

This book is dedicated to my mother, who lit the fire inside of my soul and gave me enough love for a hundred lifetimes.

Contents

Cookies

Introduction

When you spend decades building an authentic brand and putting it on the global map, you learn a thing or two. When you do it multiple times, you become an expert. I built my company, Cookies, from the ground up—and completely changed the game in the process. From my early days hustling in the streets of San Francisco to my position on top of the business world today as the founder and CEO of a billion-dollar business, I've seen what makes some companies pop and others flop.

I wear many hats: Rapper. Founder. Mogul. Trendsetter. Visionary. Cancer survivor. Father. I've built the Cookies empire the only way I know how. I'm a firm believer that big business doesn't have to be cutthroat. It just needs to be authentic and to resonate with people. That's exactly what I've done with my brands.

Now I want to show you how you can do it with yours.

People ask me for advice all the time, and my answer is always the same. Be hands-on. Be consistent. Be persistent. Invest your own money in yourself. And also, love what you do. It's that simple, and it's everything I've tried to game you up on in this book.

Whether it's my rap label, my clothing line, my creative compound, or my cannabis enterprise, I've developed some rules for how to succeed in business. At the heart of it is a commitment to staying true to yourself and your vision. In this book, I'll share the story of how I pulled it off, and I'll teach you how you can, too. Of course, there are tangible lessons I'll deliver, like how to execute a marketing campaign that stays true to you and your business, how to utilize social media to roll out your product and generate hype, and how to surround yourself with the right people to succeed.

You might already be all-in on me and the Cookies brand and are looking to read a wild story about a Mexican Italian high school dropout pursuing his dream and building an empire against all odds, or maybe you're a young entrepreneur entering the business world and looking to level up and learn from someone just like you. Either way, I got you. No matter what, I guarantee you will walk away from this book wiser and craftier than before. I may have made my name in the weed/rap/streetwear industries, but as you're about to find out, my story and the lessons I've learned straight out of the trenches are just as impactful in any emerging market or even a traditional business in desperate need of a shake-up. So roll one, put your phone on airplane mode, and prepare yourself for a billion dollars' worth of game.

—B

BECOMING Legend

SF HEMP CENTER

Chapter 1

IT STARTS WITH A VISION

I'm not sure vision is something you can learn. You either have it or you don't. I've certainly never taught anybody how to have a vision. The closest I ever come to explaining it, to helping someone learn how to be a visionary and to think bigger, is when I tell young entrepreneurs: See what you would like to exist in the world, imagine how you want things done or how you want things to be, and then execute it. A clear vision will serve as your finish line. How you get there, well, that's a whole different beast.

. . .

"*This* is the place?"

I pull up to a tiny storefront set into the street level of a gray concrete apartment building in San Francisco's Sunset District. The fog is always thick and low here, making everything seem dreamy and mysterious—just like the unmarked door I am about to enter.

It's the summer of 2001, and I'm eighteen years old, fresh off my shift at a coffee shop called Tully's where I've been working since dropping out of high school a year ago. From middle school on,

I've been hustling. I've sold everything from weed to candy bars to T-shirts to my own mixtapes. I've been trying to make a name for myself, so I'm documenting everything on a bulky handheld camcorder I picked up from a friend's kid brother. But I don't know yet how I'm going to make the next leap.

The streetlights start to turn on as I reach the Hemp Center, a medical cannabis dispensary where, amazingly, it's legal to buy weed. I heard about the Hemp Center from one of my boys, a coworker at the coffee shop. Near the end of our shifts, as we were wrapping up, he always makes these calls.

"Hey, whatup, so what you got over there today?" I'd overhear him ask.

"Oh yeah? Well, I'll take an eighth of Trainwreck, and an eighth of Romulan, and three Raspberry Bombers. Put that aside for me," he'd say. "I'll be over there in a little bit." Then we'd pool our money together and he'd head out and return with some fire—I mean, consistently great weed. It was night and day from the bland, dusty herb I smoked as a teenager in Arizona, where my family and I spent a few years before moving back to my hometown of San Francisco. As it turned out, my hometown had the best weed in the world.

. . .

I made a deep connection with weed from a relatively early age. From my first experiences smoking with my friends in grade school, I recognized the power of the plant. Sure, I liked the feeling of being high—the calm feeling of clarity I get when I smoke, the curiosity it awakens in my mind, the way time seems to slow down. And of course I enjoy the smell, the taste, and the habitual process that goes along with smoking a joint—breaking down the weed, smelling the bud in the grinder, stuffing a rolling paper full of sticky dank, and spinning it between my fingers before twisting the top and sparking that bad boy. I liken it to the way a wine connoisseur enjoys not just drinking the wine but carefully opening the bottle and sniffing the cork, pouring it into a glass and swirling it to release the aromas, and sticking their nose into the glass before tasting. But what I *really* love about weed is how it brings people together. I love that people from all different walks of life connect and bond over it. That sense of community is a big part of what keeps me smoking to this day. Plus, I've learned to love the feeling of *having* good weed, of sharing it with others and seeing the reaction it gets. There's an energy that the weed brings out in people that I gravitate to. And I love being the person who supplies that energy.

. . .

Since moving back to Cali a couple years earlier, I'd seen a few dispensaries around town. You'd see the green cross image, and I swear you could smell them from down the block. They always seemed pretty busy, but I had never been inside one. This wasn't like buying weed on the street—you needed a medical marijuana card. When I turned sixteen years old, I didn't get my driver's license. I didn't give a fuck about driving, and I still don't—these days my boy Stinje handles the driving so I can take calls, negotiate deals, handle business on my phone, and smoke big in the back seat. But you better believe that the *day* I turned eighteen I got myself a medical marijuana card and made the twenty-mile trip north to Berkeley, where there was a famously lenient doctor who would hand out marijuana permission slips like they were concert flyers.

That day, I headed straight back to San Francisco and pulled up to what I can only describe as a hole in the wall. But I was too late. The blinds were all shut, and I could see a sign reading "Closed." From the outside, it was unimpressive. Little did I know that inside was a world that would change my life forever. I returned the next morning during my first break at work. Seeing a doorbell next to the unmarked door, I nervously pressed it, still wearing the black pants and white button-down shirt we had to wear at Tully's, the black apron that completed the uniform hanging over my shoulder. I was buzzed into the Hemp Center, and from the moment I stepped through the door I could smell all that incredible fresh weed.

I showed my doctor's note to a young man at the registration desk. I could hear laughter and music coming from the other side of the wall separating the small waiting room from the dispensary. He scanned my note, checked my I.D., and assigned me a patient number—4453. I remember it to this day; it allowed them to keep a record of my transactions. He told me I could head in, and as I stepped into the main dispensary and my eyes scanned the room, one thought ran through my mind on repeat: *Holy. Shit.*

I already knew the weed was great. I'd been smoking it with my homies at work for months. But to see it up close, displayed in plastic tubs like in an ice cream shop, was wild to me. The place was intimate, roughly the size of a standard hotel suite. There was a counter where the budtenders would greet the customers. Across from it was a small green couch that could hold about four people. You could smoke your bud right then and there. I noticed that the room had a haze that lingered lazily, like the fog outside.

As I entered the room, a vendor was pulling buds out of a turkey bag from his latest batch and passing them around to the staff to sample. Nervously, I approached the counter. I glanced at the shelf and quickly ordered two grams of the first thing my eyes landed on. I could tell they had put their taste test with the vendor on pause to serve me, and I felt awkward about it. As he bagged up the product, the budtender pointed to a bowl with rolling papers in it and told me I could grab a seat on the couch and smoke one there if I wanted to.

The whole sequence of events was fucking awesome.

I don't know how else to say it other than the whole scene just felt right to me. As a kid growing up, buying, selling, holding, or smoking cannabis was always some sneaky, trappy, street, underground-type shit. The weed world I knew in my youth existed behind closed doors. But from the moment I stepped into the Hemp Center and discovered that community, that fire herb and even better vibes, I could see the future . . . and my place in it. I sat down on the couch and smoked a joint, observing as a steady stream of patients rolled in. I was impressed by the genuine camaraderie between them and the employees at the store.

It wasn't long before the Hemp Center became a part of my daily routine. I would head there right from work, grab a couple bags, and smoke a J on that green couch with my new friend, whether it be a cancer patient, a Vietnam vet, or whoever walked through those doors that day. And it was an eclectic mix, all united by a love and appreciation of fine cannabis. I was obsessed with the different strains available, what people were buying, and why they were smoking a particular strain (meaning a specific variety of cannabis plant, each possessing its own unique characteristics, from taste and appearance to the type of high you can expect to get). I was also fascinated by the whole process of where and how the Hemp Center sourced its weed: They purchased from local growers and suppliers whose products always seemed to be evolving, as breeders developed new strains and cultivators grew specific buds.

The more time I spent there, the more I grew to appreciate the vibe at the Hemp Center. I talked with the staff and the other customers, who were always referred to as "patients," and the more I spoke to them, the more I fell in love with the community. I talk a lot about "vibes." It's a big word for me; I don't care if you're a billion-dollar investor, I just can't rock with people who don't have good vibes. Well, needless to say, the vibes at the Hemp Center were loving and welcoming and felt like *Cheers* (the OGs reading this will understand that reference, but for the young cats out there, *Cheers* was the most popular show on TV when I was growing up—a sitcom about the regular patrons at a bar "where everybody knows your name"). It was so genuine and unique to any experience I'd had with weed at that point. It was special.

From my very first trip, I wanted so badly to be a part of the scene and needed an excuse to stick around for as long as possible. In some way, shape, or form, I needed to be a part of the store. During one of my first visits, I remember asking one of the budtenders if they were hiring. They were not, I was told, so I asked if I could come back the next day with my handheld video camera to make a documentary about the Hemp Center. They phoned Kathleen Gilbert, the owner, who said, "Sure, why not?" It was my first of countless experiences of turning a no into a yes.

The next day, as promised, I showed up, bulky camera and all, and began to interview the staff and the patients. Filming was how I got my foot in the door, but I also couldn't help but feel that I was witnessing history in the making and wanted to capture every moment of it. I was talking to AIDS patients who were smoking cannabis to ease the pain; to off-duty cops who needed help taking the edge off after a stressful day at work; to an eighty-year-old woman who'd tell me wild stories about getting orgasms while she danced after eating hash in Morocco; to people bravely fighting cancer; to people like myself who just appreciated good quality bud and liked getting high. I did nothing with the footage. That was my big secret at the time. Some nights, I'd watch it out of curiosity, or because I remembered an enlightening interaction with one of the customers, but for the most part, in those early days whatever I captured on my camera stayed on the tape cassette. But the more I interviewed, the more I began to see the full picture: Weed was connecting us all. It was something that people wanted, that they needed, and a whole kinship existed behind it. There was a social aspect to it that was attractive to me. More than anything, I saw that it was really helping people. I saw the bigger purpose.

As my roots in the Hemp Center and this fascinating new community grew, it struck me how normalized it all was. You have to understand that recreational cannabis was still very illegal (it would be another decade or so until that changed). All over the country, people were being jailed for smoking or possessing even small quantities. I would think, *Why did I watch friends getting arrested for smoking in Arizona, when a place like this can exist? Why isn't this available somewhere like New York City?*

In the years that followed, it became a big motivating factor for me to share the videos I'd been making online. Beginning after 2005, when platforms like YouTube launched and other video-hosting websites began gaining steam, I would edit the footage on an old desktop computer and post my interviews and vlogs to sites like YouTube and WorldStarHipHop, which was home to some of the earliest viral videos online; if you wanted a video to blow up back in those days, you posted it on WorldStar. As social media took off in the years that followed, I'd post the videos on platforms like Twitter and Facebook, where the Hemp Center and the community we were building there were beginning to attract a following. My motivation was simple: The world needed to see what was happening in California. At the Hemp Center, I would watch as the mailman would enter the main showroom full of smoke with Tupac bumping from somewhere out of view, and wouldn't even blink. It was like he was walking into any other business. *If the mailman can come in here,* I'd think, *and see me openly smoking weed, the store selling weed, and customers enjoying their medicine, and he doesn't think twice about it, then the barriers to growing this industry are practically nonexistent.*

The wheels in my head were beginning to turn as I started to see a vision where places like the Hemp Center existed all across the world. What would that look like? How would this translate to other markets? How could I, a kid without a high school diploma who had only worked entry-level jobs, make it happen? It wasn't always smooth sailing, especially as the regulatory framework around cannabis was still getting sorted out and dispensaries like the Hemp Center operated in a gray area of legality. As loving as our community was, there was a constant threat of danger from the Drug Enforcement Agency, the California Highway Patrol, and other officials coming in to seize our money. Believe it or not, that *also* attracted me to the place, this world. It meant that we were fighting for something. This wasn't just an amazing world I wanted to be a part of; a much bigger war was being waged. A fight not only for survival but for acceptance in society. I knew I needed to be a part of this war, and I damn sure knew which side I was going to be fighting on. I also knew I was going to do absolutely whatever it took to see it through and help make cannabis accessible to the masses—and accepted by mainstream society. I was hella determined, and that, more than anything, is my entrepreneurial superpower: Not quitting until I see my vision through. **It meant thinking way outside the box and finding creative ways to get things done—** from building and designing a global brand to getting a retail empire off the ground and everything in between. It hasn't been easy. I've made a career off swimming with sharks and I have the scars to prove it. Whether taking on Big Business and the corporate world or battling cancer, I'm a fighter.

And I had found something worth fighting for.

. . .

After a year of showing up every day, filming, and embedding myself in the Hemp Center, Kathleen finally relented and gave me a job; she became my mentor in cannabis. She had long been ingrained in the medical marijuana community, which we now refer to as the traditional legacy cannabis market. She had been mentored by a man named Dennis Peron, one of the most important cannabis activists in history. Peron was a Vietnam vet who later came out as gay; around 1990, during the AIDS epidemic, he began supplying AIDS patients with cannabis. In 1994 he opened a place on Market Street called the San Francisco Cannabis Buyers Club—the first real dispensary in California—and Kathleen was one of his first employees. Kathleen was extremely passionate about legalizing marijuana and fighting for the rights of cannabis users. She was an activist and took up the cause with great dedication but would occasionally confide in me that she was scared to be the face of an operation that still existed in this gray area of legality. Still, at the end of the day she didn't give a fuck; she would do whatever it took to keep the Hemp Center doors open and the dream of legal cannabis alive. Kathleen had dirty blond hair and sort of resembled Renée Zellweger circa today; at the Hemp Center she hired only young men. She ran hot and cold, but I learned that the best way to work with Kathleen was to simply be pleasant and to give her space.

Right after I was hired, she shut down that original location and moved to a bigger space on Geary Street. While the original location was small—it felt like you were in someone's living room—the spot on Geary was far more spacious and had a more commercial feel to it. It was a level-up and had a huge grow in the back. I worked there from the first day it opened, and I still consider them the best days of my life (so far). Even now I find myself dreaming of those times, crazy-vivid dreams where I'm still behind the counter helping out customers.

I leveled up quickly. I started off doing intake, which basically meant reading your doctor's note and creating your membership. From there I became a budtender (the person who takes your order and sells customers weed) before being promoted to a buyer who worked closely with growers (the farmers who cultivated the cannabis plant) and wholesalers (the mediators who purchased from growers in bulk and sold to dispensaries), helping to select the different bud we stocked, looking out for characteristics like the feel of the bud, the trichomes (the crystal-like fur on the outer layer of the bud), the smell, the taste, and the high—always striving for the best weed possible; quality has been critical for me since day one. By the time I was twenty, after just one year as an official employee, I was made store manager and put in charge of opening and closing the store.

That's when I started getting clued in as to just how profitable this shit was. I would head in for my morning shift, type in the security code, unlock the big padlock we kept on the gate, unlock the door, go inside, and pop the safe open. There'd be $100,000 cash piled up in there on any given day. It was a cash-only business back then, because no banks would work with us; most banks don't work with cash businesses. I'd continue my morning routine, put some weed out in jars, do the weigh-in, and then do inventory and whatever other paperwork needed to be done. We very much treated it like any other small business.

In California, and especially in San Francisco, after Proposition 215 was passed in November 1996, medical marijuana shops like ours were able to operate out in the open. Prop 215, which was authored by Dennis Peron, was called "the Compassionate Use Act." It permitted the use of medical cannabis in all forms (flower, edibles, oils) and allowed for places like the Hemp Center to exist on a lawful basis. We had a license to operate and were paying taxes to the state—always in cash. We also had a special license that permitted consumption as well as the ability to grow and store marijuana at our facility. The license also capped the amount of flower a patient could buy in a single day at two ounces. Honestly, it felt like, and was run like, any other legitimate business . . . for the most part.

There was always the threat of theft—and not just from street criminals. I'll never forget the day when we were raided by the California Highway Patrol. They burst through the doors, put the staff in handcuffs, and told them all to sit down on the floor. I was in the back room painting the office when I heard the commotion out front. I watched closely on the security camera feed we had set up and quickly threw a tarp over the safe. I watched as the CHP officers went through the registers and removed all the cash. Then they uncuffed everyone and left. Although we had a legal license to operate, as I said, the whole medical market existed in that gray area, so raids like that were always a possibility. Nowadays there is nothing gray about the legal weed market. To keep your doors open you must be super-compliant: Everything has to be grown in specific ways, stored a certain way, packaged and delivered to a shop a certain way—and it's all closely monitored by an army of regulators working for the Department of Cannabis Control. But back then? In the medical days, people would show up off the street with a duffel bag full of product, tell you they were a vendor, and sell their weed. I know a lot of people who were in that legacy market who miss those days. Despite our licenses, it still felt at times like we were in the Wild West.

If it wasn't the CHP giving us problems, it was sometimes my own employees. I remember opening the store one morning, and as I'm pulling product out of the safe and moving it to the display shelves, one of our oldest employees, whom we called Dirty J, sprinted through the doorway high on Oxycontin, grabbed three turkey bags of weed, and darted off. I ran out after him, only to see him heading down the block toward a van with its doors open. He tossed the bags into the van—maybe three pounds in total—and dove into the van as it sped off, tires screeching. It was straight out of a movie. Dude had the getaway car ready and everything. Thankfully our store was in a safe neighborhood, and those types of incidents were few and far between.

Day after day at the Hemp Center, I witnessed an entire industry blooming. People from all different walks of life enjoy our product. And it was *big business,* making real money. I realized that what was happening in California would inevitably spread to other places, too. At some point, I figured, cannabis would be regulated for recreational use in other states, and a massive untapped market would be created. But the most important thing I realized was, there were no brands in the space. The weed we bought and sold was mostly unlabeled, displayed in a glass jar with just the name of the strain scrawled across a piece of tape. I became totally consumed with one thought. It was my fucking mantra: *Whoever makes the first real brand in this space will win.* And I was going to do absolutely whatever I could to be that person.

That place and my experience there shaped who I am today, both as a person *and* as an entrepreneur. Those are just the facts. It's where I developed my knowledge and enhanced my love for cannabis. It was where I discovered my special purpose and the role I was going to play during my time on this Earth, outside of being a father to my kids. I was going to be somebody who brought people together and built communities based on togetherness and a shared love of this stigmatized plant that I saw firsthand can be used for so much good.

The Hemp Center is where I truly developed my Berner persona and where I began to truly blossom, serving medical marijuana customers by day and working on rap tracks in my janky, makeshift home studio by night, the whole time filming and posting each step of the journey as my following grew, slowly and organically.

It was also the place where I hooked up with a group of friends who developed incredible, groundbreaking genetics. Together, we introduced strains like Cherry Pie, Sunset Sherbet, Girl Scout Cookies, and Gelato that remain arguably the most popular cannabis products that are being bought and smoked around the world to this day; I believe that 60 to 70 percent of all cannabis on the market today has at least part of our lineage in its DNA. I used my marketing instincts and promotional skills to create a blueprint to sell cannabis to the masses. At the same time, I started my own clothing line and began making rap albums at a wild pace. The clothes, the music, the weed all fueled my Cookies empire, which today is worth billions.

What was merely a vision back in the Hemp Center's days became reality. I became the face behind the most recognized cannabis brand on the planet. The story of how it happened and the lessons I learned along the way are a master class in building a business—no matter what the enterprise or where you come from.

Cookie$
Cookies
MedEx
MedEx

Chapter 2

KNOW THE RULES BEFORE YOU BREAK 'EM

They say it's not until you step over the line that you learn exactly where the line is. This is a good way to describe my education in weed and business. There's no How to Trap *textbook, or if there is, I damn sure never read it; I learned with my eyes and ears. I was never formally taught Business 101; my schooling took place in a pre-legalization world—in the streets and in the garages, alleyways, and basements of grow houses. I was a wide-eyed kid who soaked up everything. I paid close attention to the world around me and learned the rules of the game before I was old enough to drive. That upbringing gave me a foundation that I've drawn upon in every step of my journey.*

They also say that you don't get to choose where you grow up, but looking back, I wouldn't have had it any other way. So many of my moves to this day—and the strategy behind them—are rooted in the firsthand lessons I received growing up.

Fast-forward, and my team and I created Cookies U, a two-month educational retreat at Cookies' state-of-the-art R&D facil-

ity in Humboldt County. We teach the ins and outs of the cannabis industry—every step from growing the plant to marketing and selling your product to the world. I'm giving an opportunity to the young'ns out there who, in a world before legalization, had no choice but to learn the hard way like me. The way I see it, I'm laying the groundwork so that the next generation of whales like you know which rules are meant to be followed and which rules need to be broken if you want to achieve your wildest dreams.

. . .

The three of us were crammed together in the U-Haul truck as it shook and bounced along the freeway, the sun pounding down on us. I rode shotgun, clutching my seat cushion, with Mom behind the wheel and my brother, Matt, jammed into the back seat along with everything we owned. It was the summer of 1994, and I was eleven years old, just about to start middle school as we made the eight-hundred-mile trek southeast from the Daly City, California, home I grew up in to Chandler, Arizona, where my brother and I had been told my dad had plans to open a new restaurant and a new, bigger house was waiting for us.

I was born in Children's Hospital in San Francisco in 1983 and raised in nearby Daly City, a chill, diverse suburb of San Francisco. On Skyline Boulevard, which curves around San Francisco Bay, the fog would get so thick that I swear, you could be in a high-speed chase with police right behind you and toss a baggie (or whatever) out the window, and they wouldn't be able to see a thing. It's a scene I've played out in my head a lot over the years.

I love my hometown. I grew up in a multicultural neighborhood full of flavor. You had Mexican families like mine next to Chinese families next to White, Black, Filipino, and Cambodian families. It felt communal—and it was never boring. Next door was a biker-gang house. They were cool, always had big parties going on. As kids we were always playing outside, but we never played cops and robbers; we played Crips and Bloods.

As the U-Haul snaked its way from the California seaside toward the Arizona desert, Dad, we were told, was hanging back in Daly City to wrap up some business. My dad, Gilbert, was born in California, but most all his family are from Juárez, Mexico. He had a son and daughter from a previous marriage, and I was fairly close with my half-sister, who was a few years older than me. I wasn't as close to Dad's extended family as I was with Mom's, but my great grandma on my dad's side was a phenomenal chef, and several members of his family—uncles, cousins, you name it—owned and ran restaurants in San Francisco. As anyone who has opened a restaurant will tell you, it's a grueling business, and so Dad's family were all hardworking people. I remember visiting my great grandma as a little boy and her telling me that when she was a little kid she would work all day preparing food for just a single bean-and-cheese as payment.

Dad had been in the restaurant business ever since I was born. Back then, he ran a Mexican restaurant at California and Fillmore streets, beginning a food journey that included a rotisserie chicken spot and a French fusion restaurant before he launched a catering business.

Growing up, we spent a lot of time at Dad's restaurants, and I'm glad I did. The restaurant business, I learned, is all about bartering. Day after day, I got to experience it firsthand.

"Oh, you're hungry?" Dad would ask, not waiting for the answer. "Go run across the street to Curbside Grill. Uncle Jerry is going to hook you up and put together a plate of chicken piccata for you."

He'd trade food and whatnot with other local business owners.

"You're bored? Go hit up the video store and rent a movie. Uncle Jason is going to take care of you."

It felt like some New York City shit. It was old-school, and it worked. The other business owners would come to my dad for his incredible burritos, and he'd set up credit for us around the neighborhood. We'd get pizza next door at Dino's, pasta at a spot across the street, and hit up the nearby coffee shop with the good snacks. It was a whole network he'd created. Mine wasn't the best dad when it came to being hands-on with his kids, but he still had an impact on me. I'm even named after him—my birth name is Gilbert Milam, Jr. Growing up, he'd call me "Junior." Dad was named after his father, Gilbert, and also went by "Junior," making me the third Gilbert Milam. And my toddler son, Gilbert, is the fourth. I learned how to negotiate, network, and barter watching my dad in those days. And I also learned how to leverage a situation when you have access to something people want, whether it's burritos or bud.

. . .

When Mom first told me we were moving to Chandler, I was excited for the adventure. But the ride was hell. By the time the landscape outside the window turned into dry desert, the air-conditioning had fully broken and we were all dripping sweat. About halfway through the twelve-hour trip, Mom decided to pull in at a rest-stop diner in the middle of nowhere to grab a bite and take a break from the heat.

My mom was a tough-ass woman who would do anything to take care of her family. Mom grew up in Huntington Beach, California, in your typical Italian family—the Tambarinos—and as a kid I spent plenty of time with my cousins at big family dinners enjoying some delicious meatballs, red sauce, and homemade pasta. She moved to San Francisco and worked as a headhunter and met my dad at his restaurant, where she'd go for burritos. They began dating and must have hit it off because I was born not too long after. Mom's work ethic was off the charts. As soon as we moved to Arizona, she opened her own business as a job recruiter. On the side, she also worked as a water aerobics instructor at our local YMCA. It wasn't until years later that I learned she was *also* working a newspaper delivery job to earn extra income. She never told us about it and would do her routes before we woke up in the morning. A total hustler.

From the moment we walked through the diner doors in Nowhere, Arizona, I could feel the small-town vibes and immediately felt out of place. For one thing, it seemed most everyone was White. I never thought much about being a minority in San Francisco. Everyone around was something—from brown to black to full-body-tattoo blue. I put my head down as we made our way to a booth, and I noticed people staring at us and giving us weird looks. When it came time to order, our waitress was giving Mom hella attitude. Just rude for no reason. As soon as the waitress was out of earshot, Mom told Matt and me that we were going to dine-and-dash, and that it wasn't up for debate.

As soon as we finished our meal, it was go time. She pulled out a few dollar bills, flipped over a full glass of water, and placed the bills under the cup. "That'll make it look like we left a tip," she said. "That waitress is going to be too busy cleaning up this mess to realize we haven't paid." I looked around nervously. She stood up, grabbed a bottle of hot sauce and the salt and pepper shakers from the table, and tossed them into her purse with a smile on her face. I begged her not to, but it was no use. She'd already made up her mind. That was Mom: the sweetest person in the world—until she felt she needed to be spiteful.

The notoriously relentless Arizona sun beat down on the U-Haul as we pulled into the driveway of our new home in Chandler. There had recently been a monsoon in the area, and I still remember the smell of the wet grass from the driveways as we arrived. Our new home was a cookie-cutter house in a new development, beige stucco with a Spanish tile roof, like all the other ones on the street, lined up row after row. There was a swimming pool in the backyard and three bedrooms, which meant that Matt and I wouldn't have to share a room anymore. We'd barely made it three steps into the door when Mom shut it behind us.

"Boys," she said abruptly. "I need to talk to you. Your father isn't coming."

She broke the news to us. She had caught him cheating on her and had decided to seek a divorce. She explained it all very matter-of-factly, brushing it off and letting us know that we were going to be OK. If she was heartbroken or afraid, she put on a brave face and didn't show us. It's one of the million reasons why I still consider Mom the strongest person I've ever met. She kissed Matt and me on the forehead and told us she loved us. Then we ran into the backyard and jumped into the pool with all our clothes on.

. . .

We were starting from scratch, and it felt like it. Looking around at Chandler, everything was different than Daly City. I had left a community that was a perfect alphabet soup of weirdness and cool and had landed in a place that was, with the exception of the odd Mexican, very White and boring. *Where the fuck am I?* I thought to myself as I looked up and down our street at all the uniform houses.

It felt like some *Twilight Zone* shit. There were a few kids playing outside, but everyone kept to themselves. I wondered how I'd ever make friends.

On our first full day in town, Mom must have sensed that we were bored and suggested that we walk to Walgreens to pick up some snacks. Cool. We started walking, and some guy driving by must've seen my black, slicked-back hair because he rolled down his window and yelled "Fuckin' beaner!" and threw an egg at me. Welcome to Arizona. I don't ever like to put myself in a box, but I've always been proud of my Latino roots. My dad spoke Spanish around the house, and I cherished growing up in Mexican restaurants and around that culture. I've never thought too heavy on it, but being in Chandler was definitely making me more aware of who I was.

Later that day the rains began to fall again. It was like nothing I'd ever seen. Gallons and gallons came pouring down, and in no time our entire street was flooded. I stepped out into the middle of the road, the water up past my ankles, and soaked it in.

Still, I spent those early days feeling scared and alone. With the first school semester around the corner, I didn't think I'd ever find homies, let alone ones who were cool and tapped in. At first my classmates called me "Crisco," because of my slicked-back hair, which was the popular style back in Daly City. When they found out I was from San Francisco, they also started making jokes about *Full House* and Rice-A-Roni, and called me "gay"—all the San Fran stereotypes coming at me at once.

But those early awkward days didn't last long, and soon I found my way into a small crew of friends: Bear, Eli, and Ruben. In my school, kids had to fit into one of three categories: jocks, gangsters, or goths. We were gangsters, and we didn't need to look far to find our role models. All three of my new homies had older brothers who were notorious hustlers in and around Chandler. They drove cars with nice rims. They wore big gold chains. They smoked weed and listened to rap music. They were swagged out, larger than life. And we wanted to be just like them.

Ruben's older brothers were active in the streets, especially his oldest bro, Sergio. I'll never forget the first time I met him. He was wearing a giant Turkish gold chain with an ornate gold cross dangling from it. It was just like a chain I remembered seeing Tupac wearing in an interview on MTV. Pac was a hero of mine. We all loved him. I told Sergio I was from the Bay, and I knew who the underground rappers were in that scene—guys like E-40 and B-Legit, who were featured on Pac's *All Eyez on Me*. That seemed to impress him and his friends, and they started to vibe with me.

Ruben's brothers sold weed all over town. They would keep it in the garage of their family home, garbage bags filled with bales of cheap Mexican weed. One day we worked up the courage to grab a big handful out of one of the bags. We crammed it into a Ziploc baggie and took it to school. Huddled around my locker, each of us shoved a hand into the bag, ripped off a piece of the weed, and munched on it like it was Big League Chew. We didn't know how to get high. We were just kids, twelve or thirteen, chewing weed like it was bubble gum.

I really looked up to Bear's big brother, Benny. That's who I wanted to be. Benny always seemed calm and collected. He was short and stocky but in good shape, always rocking gold chains and bracelets. He drove a '64 Chevy Impala and was a hustler's hustler. One day we were hanging around Benny's place, and he came up to us.

"What up, dudes? Y'all wanna make some money?" he asked, a twinkle in his eye. "Or you wanna go to school and do nothing?"

We followed him into his room, which was full of boxes of candy bars. "Take this candy and go slang it," he said. *Slang it?* I didn't know what he meant.

"Look," he explained. "I'll give it to you for this price, then you go sell it for a higher price. You bring me back X dollars, then you can keep the rest." He was training us—giving us game, you might say—but it was also a test to see who he could trust. Who is going to take this candy, sell it, and bring the money back? And which one of these little dudes is going to just eat it? Let's be real: You gotta be strict to be a kid and not eat that shit. I passed with flying colors.

It wasn't long before I was graduating from selling candy, fast-tracked to a master's program in hustling. Within a few months, Benny was fronting us sheets of acid to sell at school. "I'll give you this entire sheet for a hundred bucks," he'd explain, pulling out what looked like a sheet of paper with a hundred perforated stamps on it. "You sell each one for five bucks and you can make five hundred bucks. You do that, you come back here, give me one hundred and keep four hundred."

Me and my friends quickly became known by our schoolmates as the kids who could get you weed and acid. I fell in love with the popularity—being wanted was a high of its own—and I took quick note that exclusive access to something others want was the first step in learning the game.

. . .

Benny's house was like a chapel compared to my buddy Eli's. It turned out that Eli was living in a stash house. His father and uncles were running dope for the Mexican cartels, and they figured that having kids and a seemingly normal family living in the stash house was the perfect cover. At Eli's, there was weed everywhere. We were taught to bring pounds of weed into the bathroom and let the shower run and then watch the steam help the compact weed expand. Eli's family would smoke around him, and I'll never forget one of his relatives coming around at the holidays with special shit he called Christmas Chronic. We smoked that stuff with Eli's dad, who explained how, because it was exclusive and only came to town once a year, you could charge a lot more for it. I was still too green to get exactly what made it superior, but I took note.

We would steal some of the regular weed to smoke ourselves, which led to Eli's uncles intervening. "Fuck stealing," one of them said. "Why don't you work for us and smoke for free?"

When it came to selling, I was a quick study. A total natural, you might say. I earned the trust of Eli's family quickly, and before I knew it I was joining them on weekend trips to a border town called Ajo. Eli's mom and dad would sit up front, with Eli and his girlfriend, Kelly, a White girl with blond hair and blue eyes, and me sitting in the back.

Much later, I found out that they were running serious stuff on those trips. Cocaine or cash, I think. Definitely not weed, which wouldn't have fit in the trunk of their small sedan.

The first time we arrived in Ajo, I remember we met up with Eli's cousin, who told Eli and me he'd just found a bale of weed in the desert. He cut off a piece and said he'd give it to us for twenty bucks. It was probably worth like three hundred bucks, but none of us knew what we were doing. We wrapped it up in baggies and put them in our backpacks to bring back home. Eli's dad had brought us on this trip to throw off the cops and make it look like a regular weekend getaway, normal family shit. But meanwhile we were packing our bags with all this smelly weed. Our amateur trafficking antics might have ruined everything for them.

But I was hooked, fully immersed in the weed game. I loved being someone other people needed, somebody important. And the way I could leverage access to cannabis to grow my status was more addicting than any drug I tried.

One day we were hanging around Ruben's place when someone brought some new weed. He said it was called Purple Kush and claimed it came from California. I didn't even know there was a difference. The Cali weed, this guy explained, was $20 per gram. I tried to keep a straight face. The Mexican brick weed all of us sold cost $25 for an *ounce*.

I think Ruben's brothers were offended by the hype surrounding the Purple Kush, which made their shit look weak in comparison. Sergio dipped one of the dark green buds in alcohol and announced that it was fake, covered in some type of artificial coloring. ("Maybe even nail polish," he said.) That brought the hype train to a crashing halt. It was back to business as usual—or so I thought.

. . .

Despite being regularly burned by hot seat buckles—on a hot day you could fry an egg on the street—I was falling in love with Arizona and especially my crew of homies. When summer came around, I was actually depressed to have to leave to go back to San Francisco to visit my dad, who had moved out of our former home in Daly City and into a studio apartment above his restaurant at Fillmore and California streets.

The place was hella small. You walked in and there was a bathroom immediately to your left, a small hallway leading to a single room with a small kitchen and a fire escape that I'd sit out on and smoke weed. It was me, my brother, my dad, and my dad's friend Jerry, the chef from Curbside, all staying there together. Jerry would sleep in the hallway, his feet by the bathroom door and his head in the living room. Dad slept on a pullout couch, while Matt and I found some space on the floor. To take a piss in the middle of the night, I'd have to step over Jerry. He never seemed to mind.

While I was back in town, I took the opportunity to visit my old friend Ray, a Filipino kid who was my best friend growing up. We were always hanging out, and I was curious how he'd been since I left town.

Dad dropped me off at Ray's house one afternoon. I noticed the garage was cracked open slightly. As I approached, the pungent and unmistakable smell of weed punched me in the face. My nostrils filled with the loud scent, and I could feel the fireworks going off in my brain. It smelled like some sort of SuperWeed, unlike anything I'd ever smelled before. I noticed Ray's older brother, Anthony, sitting down with his hands inside a tackle box that was resting on his lap. I said "Whatup" and let him know how good that weed smelled. He was shocked that I smoked or knew anything about weed, but he told me that he and his friends were about to hotbox his car if I wanted to join. I was there to see Ray, so I passed.

It's funny how quickly people can grow apart. In a matter of minutes, I could tell that Ray and I had nothing in common anymore. We chatted for a bit—I don't really remember much of it except that Ray confided in me that he thought he might be gay, which took a lot of strength. Still, over the previous year in Arizona, my whole world had changed. I wanted to be a hustler; I wanted wealth and notoriety. Ray wanted to be a kid. At the time, Pogs were really popular—these little round cardboard discs you would collect and try to flip over with a heavy plastic disc called a slammer. Ray just wanted to play with his Pogs. But I was too busy talking about the smell of Anthony's weed. I was excited, and I started to tell Ray about what I'd been up to in Arizona and the weed hustle I was getting a firsthand education in.

"If you're so into weed," Ray said, clearly annoyed, "then you should just go downstairs and hang out with Anthony and his friends." So I did.

I was at a crossroads. Ray wanted to play games and hang out like we were still in the sixth grade. But I felt like I'd been elevated past that kid stuff. As a parent, I look back on it now and realize that in Arizona I had grown up too fast. Way too fast. Pogs? Hopping on the bike and going to 7-Eleven to get Slurpees? Fuck that. That world was gone. I wanted to get high.

I headed down the stairs. The smell of burnt weed was strong, and I had to see what it was all about. In Anthony's room, he opened the tackle box and sold his friend a quarter ounce, around seven grams, for $100. My jaw hit the floor. In Arizona, I told him, a quarter *pound* was $100. "Grab a seat," he said, tossing me a quarter-ounce bag. I didn't know it at the time, but this was the moment that truly changed my life. It gave me a new level of thinking. This was the day I first saw the bigger picture, a whole galaxy of opportunities that good strong high-quality cannabis could unlock.

I didn't need to even open the bag to smell it. The light, fluffy green buds seemed to glow through the bag, and I noticed residue smears from all the tiny crystal-like hairs that cover the outside of the bud (which I later learned were called trichomes). The weed, Anthony explained, was indoor-grown California hydroponics, an effective growing method using water and light that doesn't require soil. I had never seen anything like it before. He began to describe the bud and explain the telltale signs of the good stuff. "See the bright lime-green color? See the crystals?" he said. "And the little orange hairs? Smell that funk?" he continued. "Notice how there are no seeds and very few stems?" It was goddamn beautiful.

Next thing I knew, Anthony handed me a joint from the tackle box. I took a dry pull on the joint before lighting it and got a taste of fresh mango with a funky skunk-like smell that lingered—nothing like the tasteless weed I was smoking back in Chandler. That weed was what we called brick weed. It was so compressed and full of stems and seeds that you had to break it down in a shoebox, let all the seeds fall to the bottom, and then pick them out, like you were prospecting for gold. It was brownish in color—nothing like this brilliant green—and barely had any aroma except for maybe a hint of gasoline from when it had been transported from Mexico. Around this time, people were way more used to smoking the "brick weed." It was mainly in small pockets of the country—Humboldt County in California, for example, along with parts of Oregon, Washington, and Colorado—where the super high-quality bud was being developed. A new generation of growers was emerging that had absorbed the secrets to growing great weed from the OGs but also relied on new tools like internet forums. Still, most of the country was smoking shwag.

Going from that to Anthony's weed was like going from eating a dry plain hamburger to taking a bite of bomb-ass Wagyu with some ponzu-style sauce drizzled on it. As far as I'm concerned, Anthony's was the first *real* weed I ever tasted. I couldn't wait to tell my boys back in Chandler.

We kicked back and watched Master P's *I'm Bout It,* a cult classic where the rapper plays a drug dealer in Louisiana. I laughed uncontrollably damn near the whole way through and went back home that night with one thought in my mind: *I gotta figure out a way to bring this back to Arizona.*

. . .

With the last of my summer spending money, I was able to buy a quarter ounce from Anthony just before I was set to fly back to Chandler for the start of the school year. I bagged it into fourteen half-gram baggies. I loved the look and feel of those baby bags filled to each corner with the sticky California weed. I stuffed them into an empty Newport cigarette box. Needless to say, the airplane cabin reeked of exotic skunk the whole flight. When we landed and I felt the desert heat during the walk to baggage claim, the excitement really kicked in. I was about to be the fuckin' *man.*

I had it all planned out. The mission, in my mind, was simple. I had fourteen bags, each one with enough weed for one blunt. I needed one for each of Ruben, Bear, and Eli's house and one for school. That would expose a ton of people to this shit, and with that hype I could sell seven bags, make my money back, and still have three bags left over to smoke with the boys.

An old brown Cadillac pulled up to the curb. It was Bear and his cousin.

"Damn, fool," Bear said as I got into the back seat and we drove off. "You smell wild." He turned around to look at me, sparking a blunt as he raised an eyebrow.

"You bring something back with you?"

I smiled from ear to ear.

"Put that blunt down."

. . .

We arrived at Ruben's. He was ironing and creasing his jeans in the front room when we walked in. I could hear unreleased 2Pac tapes coming from upstairs. I got out the Newport box and told him to call his brothers. I wanted them to see this first. We gathered around the kitchen counter and stared at the bud. Unlike the Purple Kush, *nobody* was questioning if this was fake.

We cracked a Swisher Sweet, rolled the half gram, and passed it around like a trophy. One skinny-ass blunt had all six of us loaded and laughing.

And just like that, I had the good shit. I loved the feeling. I still do. I don't need to be the biggest dog in the room; I wanted to be the most important dog in the room. That's a high of its own. My mindset was: *You could have a $500K car, $300K worth of jewelry, the baddest bitch in the world, and a bank account full of money . . . but you ain't got this weed right here.* I loved that this was going to open doors for me. I liked being the one who had the thing nobody else had. As the high began to wear off, Sergio asked me how many baggies were left in the box. I told him thirteen, and he pulled out three $100 bills, slapped them on the counter, and put the Newport box in his pocket. I was stoked I'd tripled my money, but my plan to show this Cali weed to everybody I knew was officially fucked.

"Actually, wait. I need that back," I told him. He pulled out one of the half-gram baggies, threw it over to me, and left. Deflated, me and Bear and his cousin rolled up another blunt and got silly high in the brown Cadillac and ended our night at Burger King.

I was learning the true lesson of limited supply. Having that Cali weed was like holding the conch in *Lord of the Flies*. Only he who holds it is allowed to speak, and everybody else has to listen. Two months after introducing the weed to Sergio and them, I was back in the Bay to visit my dad, though all I *really* cared about was bringing more weed back to Arizona with me than last time. I bought a quarter pound—four ounces—wrapped it in plastic wrap, and covered it in Vaseline, thinking it would cover the smell. I cut a slit in a sock and put the weed inside and had the sock inside my shorts. Dad drove me to the airport. At one point during the ride he patted me on the leg and felt the sock. He gave me a worried look, but I could tell he wasn't sure what to say. He didn't say anything. But needless to say, Dad knew why I was so nervous on the way to the airport.

This felt way riskier than last time. While I was in line at the check-in counter, I felt a knot in my stomach and went to the bathroom and vomited. Then I called Dad and asked him to pick me up. I took another flight the next day. This time I wore baggy pants and wrapped the shit up better. I still felt like I was having a heart attack the whole flight, because the plastic wrap didn't do shit. The whole Southwest plane smelled like a skunk.

In the meantime, it turned out that not only had Sergio been showing those bags to all the right people, but he'd been doing me right by telling his homies that I was the one who could get it from the Bay. Sergio was creating hype, demand, and interest (all lessons I took on). And he was making me more valuable in the process.

People started asking if, on my next trip to the West Coast, they could get their hands on some of that Cali weed. It wasn't long before I was outgrowing my plug—my connection. All the excitement, I realized, was based off the access I had to Anthony, and to something brand-new that nobody had ever seen before. Hella hype + access to high-quality goods = high demand. That spark, from my eighth-grade mind, is part of why I market everything from clothing to herb the way I do today. I've used the same tactics and principles while building a billion-dollar business.

Here's a quick lesson: For something to be *hot,* there has to be *hype*. Create a demand. A sense of urgency. Since launching Cookies, I've seen multiple companies in the space mimic the blueprint that helped us explode onto the scene. They hire celebrities to promote their products in the hope it will help reach real smokers. But it doesn't work, because they aren't growing the kind of authentic buzz you need to succeed in the cannabis industry. And this lesson translates to any emerging industry or business aimed at the culture. Let's be real: There's nothing cool about a paid ad on Instagram or a forced partnership with zero passion or know-how.

Don't get me wrong—celebrities can make a world of difference, and there's no question that access to people like Wiz Khalifa and Snoop Dogg made a major difference in my success. But whether it's a rapper or a powerful businessman, you need to know how to use that access. In the music business, for example, they know how to build hype. You'll hear artists brag about their limited-edition sneakers, their one-of-one diamond chain or custom car, their exclusive clothing drops that the average kid in America would have to wait in lines for hours or days for the chance to buy. In the process, the demand grows.

. . .

Visiting my dad more had left me daydreaming about moving back to the Bay Area. I loved hanging with my Chandler crew, but I was starting to feel over Arizona.

It was another annoyingly hot day in Chandler when I decided to open my heart up to my mom. She cooked me up my favorite pasta, a ricotta-stuffed shell, and during a long, heartfelt conversation at our kitchen table, I explained to her I had outgrown Chandler and was beginning to feel boxed in in that suburban environment. To me, a typical 9–5 job meant a boring existence, and that wasn't an option. Going to jail for something I loved felt more and more likely, and the feeling of being stuck in Arizona, with limited reach, sucked. I wanted nothing to do with it.

The weed, but also everything else interesting in San Francisco that was missing in Chandler, I swear, it was calling my name. I was just starting to get into music and had been performing a bit in the underground rap scene in Arizona, but I wanted to give getting into the music game a serious shot. Back home I felt I could have access to the people, tools, and rooms where I could at least put myself in a position to succeed. I needed the Bay, which at the time was considered a major center for independent rap music. Of course, being in the tenth grade, I also still needed my mother and the roof she put over my head. As much as I enjoyed the freedom that came with staying at Dad's place, it was pretty obvious that his studio apartment wasn't a long-term solution. Between bites of her signature pasta, I told Mom how I wanted to get back to my roots and really wanted to chase my dreams and to establish myself in the Bay Area scene. I explained how if I stayed in Arizona, my chances of making it were less than zero. We spoke for what must have been hours. Mom mostly listened. She told me she supported me and appreciated my honesty. That day I learned the power of real conversation, because in no time Mom was researching places to rent in San Francisco. After the kind of mischief I was getting into, I'm sure she was happy for me to get a change of scenery, but to move my brother and me was no small task, especially to an expensive place like the Bay. I know that was a major life decision that she made for me. We didn't have the money to afford San Francisco and its notorious cost of living. But what can I say? Mom was my superhero, and she made it happen.

We found a house on 31st and Pacheco in a predominantly Chinese neighborhood in the Sunset District. There were awesome restaurants nearby and public transportation just two blocks from our front door. It was cultural. It was urban. It was home. It was perfect. I even got the in-law suite down in the basement, which made me feel like I was living in my own bachelor pad and gave me the space I needed to be creative and smoke massive amounts of weed, which I did. After all, now that I was back in California I was living in a gold mine of cannabis.

At first, I was enrolled at Galileo High School, which didn't exactly have the best reputation and proved to be an influential place for me even if I was getting more and more uninterested in my classes with each passing day. In fact, Galileo is where I first got my name, Berner. At my new school, I sought out the rebels or outcasts—the "gangsters"—just as I had when I first moved to Chandler. What can I say, those were my people. One of my earliest friends at Galileo was a graffiti artist who went by the alias "Burner." I had also gotten into tagging and loved the creative aspect of graffiti art as much as I loved the feeling of getting away with tagging up the side of a building. My buddy Burner lived in a really rough neighborhood called Hunters Point. He lived in the projects and would describe to me scenes of packs of dogs running loose near his house, people he knew being killed every day. He said every time he stepped out of his door he felt like he was constantly looking over his shoulder, and I know he found some comfort leaving his hood and hanging out with someone like me, who by comparison came from a more stable environment. We'd skip school and hang out, smoking blunts and drinking 40s of Steel Reserve. Burner was my homie and seriously gifted with a spray can in his hands; I looked up to him as a graffiti artist. But Burner was going through some dark stuff at home. He never told me details beyond saying something like "things aren't great," but I could just tell he was dealing with some real pain.

"Listen," he told me one day, out of the blue. "I think I'm about to be saved. I'm going Christian."

"What the hell?" I asked, genuinely shocked. Needless to say, our lifestyle didn't exactly scream "Christian values."

"Yeah, blood. I'm serious," he replied. "I'm giving up graffiti and everything."

"Damn," I said, before blurting out the first thought that came to my mind. "Can I have the Burner name?"

I had always liked the name and instinctively felt that I could do a lot with it. Plus it was hella on-brand for me, because back in those days I was putting this shitty hash into my joints and pieces of lit hash were always falling out of the cherry—the glowing hot ember—and leaving small burn marks on my clothes.

He didn't hesitate when he said yes, and with his blessing I adopted the name, changing it from "Burner" to "Berner" to help make it my own.

To make some spending money, I would buy an ounce from Anthony for $300 and divide it up into twenty-eight little bags with a gram or so in them, and my little brother Matt and me would sell those for $20 each to the tourists who would hit Haight Street, famously once the hippie capital of the world and the epicenter of peace, love, and rock 'n' roll. But those days were long gone, and the neighborhood had become a tourist haven as well as a one-stop shop for drugs of all kinds. The tourists all wanted to come to the home of the hippies and, as part of their experience, get some good bud while they were there. Matt was a super bright kid but had always been more reserved than me; I was big and bold, never afraid to approach random strangers and strike up a conversation. Matt and I worked well together, and we'd both gotten the gift of gab from our mother and an understanding of the art of the transaction from watching our father run his restaurant.

By this time, Mom had gotten Matt and me transferred to a better school, Lincoln High School at 24th Avenue, just south of Quintara Street, in the hopes we would start to take our classes more seriously. But in reality, we just saw it as another opportunity to sell weed to a new customer base.

Anthony's weed, just like when I first tried it, was still fire—high-end, quality herb from Humboldt County. At that time the two main strains coming out of there were called Super Skunk and Salmon Creek Big Bud. The buds were big, fluffy, funky, and covered in trichomes. The kids at our high school were loving it and buying the $20 baggies as fast as we could prepare them.

Matt and I were walking home from school one cloudy day when the roar of engines drowned all other sounds out. I turned around just as what felt like twenty (but was probably more like four or five) Honda Civics pulled up and surrounded me. In our neighborhood, it was common knowledge that the Asians ran the drug game, and before I ever got a look at the cars I heard the aftermarket exhaust pipes barking and knew the sound was coming from what everyone in the Sunset District referred to as "rice rockets"—souped-up matching Civics with large spoilers and comically large exhaust pipes sticking out of the back that the local Asian crews drove. These guys were running what I found to be an incredibly interesting program. At places like Lincoln High School, the Asians had basically been the only game in town, selling exclusively two good-not-great strains called Pineapple and Mango (it was nothing like Anthony's weed, though). I can't share the exact details, but let's just say they never worried about running dry and basically had a never-ending supply. But their operation went way beyond local high schools and tourist traps. These guys were quite sophisticated; they had set up a pager system that you might remember if you came of age in the Bay Area in the early 2000s. You called a pager and typed in a three-digit number on the keypad.

You would receive an immediate response with an intersection and a time—almost never more than fifteen minutes from when you contacted them. Then you would stand at the intersection until a souped-up Honda Civic—a rice rocket—pulled up. You'd hop in the back seat of the car and place your order while one of the Asian dudes in the passenger seat retrieved the amount of weed you wanted from a backpack at his feet. The driver would circle the block, drop you off at the original intersection, and disappear into the fog as if none of it had ever happened. They were notorious, and I recognized the Civics the moment they approached me. The cars emptied out, and in a matter of seconds we were surrounded by at least ten guys, all wearing these fancy leather jackets and The North Face gear. We were badly outnumbered, and you could tell by the cold, serious looks on their faces that these guys meant business.

One of them, clearly the leader of this group, came up to Matt and me and began to tell us that he was very upset. (I later found out his name was Marvin.) He was pissed off that we had been selling at the school. Our awesome weed was disrupting their business. We had shit on smash.

Who could blame them? I thought. Their weed was mass-produced, which inevitably is going to lead to lower quality, or at the very least less quality control. Anthony's, on the other hand, was cultivated in small batches from a grower he knew in Humboldt County, an agricultural hot spot a few hours north of San Francisco.

In the corner of my eye I saw one of them reach into his coat pocket and I knew for sure we were about to be robbed—or worse.

Marvin continued to remind us that the school was part of their territory as my eyes darted around looking for an escape route.

The next thing I knew, Matt was cutting Marvin off. I don't

know how he manned up so fast, but out of nowhere, and with the confidence of a seasoned negotiator, he asked, "How much would you front us a quarter pound for?"

I couldn't believe what I was hearing. *"Front us"?* Matt was speaking like a true drug dealer, asking essentially how much we'd have to pay them back if they gave us a quarter pound to sell at school. I mean, you've got to remember that we were still kids buying just a few ounces at a time. This felt like more than we could handle at the time. Plus, they were already selling the same weed at our school—they were doing just fine without us. I was shocked and confused, but Matt was not only defusing the situation but turning the tables on them.

"Huh?" Marvin cocked his head to the side and studied my brother, who remained as cool as the Sunset District breeze. Even Marvin couldn't believe it.

"A quarter pound," Matt repeated. "How much?"

Marvin looked at the homies.

"Nine hundred," he said. "And we can drop it off to you today. But there's one condition: Stop bringing that other shit to school."

"Deal," said Matt.

On the rest of the walk home, I was furious at him. "How the fuck are we going to sell a *quarter pound*? And where in the world are you going to find *nine hundred dollars* if we don't?"

"Gil," Matt said to me, "remember how Anthony said he was having some trouble with his supplier?" He was right. The last few times we tried buying weed from Anthony, he said he had to wait a week or two until his supplier in Humboldt County could deliver. Although Anthony's weed was without question better than what the Asians had, any weed is better than no weed. "Let's just sell this quarter pound to Anthony." I looked Matt up and down and couldn't wipe the smile from my face. I was a proud big bro that day.

Later that night, I got the quarter pound from the Asians and went over to visit Anthony. He was still waiting for his supplier, said the price on the Asian's weed was right, and also mentioned that this plug—or hookup—could be helpful for him going forward for anytime he found himself in this same situation of essentially being forced to pause his business because of factors outside his control. Anthony even gave me an extra hundred bucks. When I returned the $900 to Marvin the next day, he was super juiced at how quickly we'd turned the product around and delivered the money. I ended up becoming pretty close with Marvin, and he helped to game me up in those early years. He would teach me about the cannabis supply chain and the importance of staying on top of your operation. The Asians took their business seriously. They respected their customers, were never robbed, and didn't play games. They were incredibly organized. They were the truth. And I learned a ton from seeing their approach up close.

It was a wild experience to go from all I saw in Arizona to this. It felt like I'd gone from swinging on the monkey bars at the local park to competing in the Olympics. It was a completely new ballgame. I was leveling up, soaking in all the knowledge I could about the underground weed game and taking mental notes each step of the way.

For a long time, I used to think back to those teenage years and chalk it all up to being reckless and wild—the kind of irresponsible childhood I would never want for my own kids. But today I revisit all these moments and recognize the countless lessons I picked up along the way:

- Quality matters. No matter the product or service, people can tell the difference between good and poor quality, often instantly.

- Access to quality product not only gives you an advantage over your competitors but also opens doors for you.
- Demand grows *quickly* if you have something perceived as exclusive that everybody wants to get their hands on.
- Don't be afraid to be yourself. You might not fit into a cookie-cutter mold, and that's probably a good thing. Work to identify the things that make you special and the skills and vision that only you can bring to the table.
- Sometimes you need to take major risks to make major waves.
- A powerful idea can come from any source, no matter how unexpected.
- If you are passionate about what you are selling, then people will recognize that and it will help you build credibility through authenticity.

All of this was ingrained in me from a young age, stayed with me all these years, and has been at the core of my success. My upbringing was more than a coming of age; it was a long education in how to hustle. And you better believe I've carried these lessons with me on my journey to become the face and foundation of not just a globally recognized brand but an entire industry.

Cookie$

$
SF
SF HEMP C
TULLY'S
COFFEE
SF
jelly's
BUDTENDER
BARISTA
BARTENDER

Chapter 3

EMBRACE THE MULTI-HYPHENATE

A big change over the generations is that these days you see countless young entrepreneurs wearing many hats at once. From the outside it can look like a messy, confusing, nonlinear journey—and a lot of times it is. But that's just the reality of the hustler's life today. Some of you may be working at an IT call center during the day while making music at night and delivering for DoorDash in your free time. Or some other multi-hyphenate game you've got going not just to make money but to pursue your dreams.

It was the same for me. I didn't fully Steve Jobs it from the Hemp Center to Cookies. My path zigzagged way more than that. I had a lot of different things going on at the same time—I had my 9–5 while trying to start clothing and accessories lines, trapping, writing and recording my own music, and putting the wheels in motion for a fire cannabis brand in Cookies. To some, these things may seem counterproductive, or at least strange or random. But you have to understand, there were no rules for a Mexican American high school dropout to be a CEO who was on the cover of Forbes *magazine. Just as there were no rules in the legal weed game at the time.*

So I had to make them up as I went along, and each path played a part in fueling the other: Rapping built my connections and my understanding of the power of social media, while also building my confidence in front of people and giving clarity to my voice and persona. Designing and selling T-shirts and hoodies eventually unlocked how to grow the Cookies brand, creatively trademark the name, and help market and add value to my name while putting walking billboards for Cookies on people's bodies.

Think about those old images of men leaving for work in the morning to waste away in the same job for their whole career—a job that started right after college and ended at some sad retirement party at Benihana. Now think about how much the world around you has changed. These different paths aren't an accident. They are the point. They all contain their own lessons and connections and ideas. It's this soup that nourishes you, and you will soon learn to get rid of the ingredients that don't add much to the recipe. Don't just throw stuff away because it doesn't seem to add up to a definition of a "career," because chances are, you won't realize how much those different flavors have helped shape the killer gumbo you've become.

That multi-hyphenated hybrid hustle is what being an entrepreneur today is all about. As you work different angles, you'll discover your superpower and what is missing in the equation that you and only you can solve for. And it may involve only one of the many paths you've been following. Or, in my case, all of them.

. . .

In my senior year I dropped out of high school. School wasn't for me. In class—when I was in class—I'd either be doodling on my notebook, workshopping potential graffiti designs and different ways I could tag the name *Berner,* or daydreaming about how I was going to leave my mark on the world. I was making some noise selling weed at school and to tourists, and I was leveling up working with and learning from Marvin. I was making progress as an artist; I had really gotten into creating designs that could jump from the pages of my notebook to public-facing walls for everyone in the city to see. I also began listening to music with more intention than before, and I was beginning to dive into what was a blossoming hip-hop scene in the Bay. I couldn't see how any of that would lead to a career, but it didn't matter. All of it I found way more interesting and engaging than anything we were doing in my classes. I knew that school was for many people, and that I was just not one of those people. I was distracted and eager to get some real-life experience under my belt. I had landed a job on the weekends, bar backing at a local establishment called Jelly's that a friend of my dad's owned. Even though it was basic labor—polishing glasses, slicing limes, hauling the occasional keg, and chatting with customers—I loved the feeling of being grown-up and the responsibility that came with showing up and being on time. I told Mom my decision, explained how I could do far more good in the world outside of the classroom. She understood; she was already clued in that school wasn't my thing. She made a deal with me: I could drop out so long as I got a second job to fill my time on the weekdays. I agreed before she could even finish the sentence.

Within a couple of weeks, I had landed a job at Tully's Coffee in Cole Valley, at the corner of Cole Street and Carl Street, a few blocks from Haight-Ashbury. I fit in right away and found out very quickly that every one of my managers smoked weed. It wasn't long before I was selling herb to all of them, and before I knew it, I was dealing to damn near all the businesses on the block. It started with my co-workers. I would bring some weed around, show them the sticky light-green exotic bud, and tell them to give it a smell and notice the hint of grape or any other notable characteristics.

Then my managers became my customers. One of them would say, "Oh, you know, Bob at the burger joint down the street would love this."

"Well, shit," I'd respond. "Tell them to slide by on their break and come find me."

Before long, the staff of a nearby burger shop, postal workers from the closest post office, architects from a local architecture firm, and even employees at the toy shop next door were all coming into Tully's on a near-daily basis to buy weed. My managers were aware and totally cool with it. At my station where I served customers, I would keep empty Tully cups under the counter with baggies of eighths (an eighth of an ounce is a hair over 3.5 grams) I sold for $50 each underneath one cup, and quarter-ounce bags I sold for $100 under another.

Life was good. I was making real money—earning a paycheck from Tully's, a paycheck from Jelly's, tips from both, and about $200 every time I sold an ounce worth of weed—plus I was smoking for free and living debt-free. At the time, I was still buying large amounts of weed to sell from Marvin and the Asians and smaller amounts from Anthony to smoke myself or to show off. Once I became a patient at the Hemp Center, I started buying my shit from there and reselling it to my growing customer base at Tully's.

I fell into a routine; my morning commute to Tully's became a highlight of my day. I'd step out of my front door, turn right, and walk for about eight blocks through residential streets to catch the

5 A.M. N Judah train from Mom's place in the Sunset District to the Cole-Ashbury neighborhood I worked in. It would be pitch black, super calm and quiet, and you could see the fog lit up by the streetlamps. I'd spark a joint, throw on headphones, and listen to some Bay Area rap or something I had recorded myself. I guess you could say I was learning what I could do better the next time I got behind a microphone. As I passed the homes, the pungent smell of weed seemed to be coming from damn near all of them. I later learned that the Sunset was full of household grow-ops, like a mini–Humboldt County. I don't know exactly what it was about those walks—the brief moment of solitude before a day full of interacting and engaging with people, maybe, or the exclusive feeling of being up and about before most of my neighbors were even awake—but I fucking cherished it. I'd step onto that train, listening to my tunes with a good high, ready for whatever the day had in store for me.

I was in a nice groove. On weekdays I slung coffee and weed at Tully's and on Friday, Saturday, and Sunday nights I worked at Jelly's. In my spare time, I began writing music—very basic stuff—and would find free instrumentals online. Using my old shitty desktop computer and a microphone I bought at a Guitar Center, I would make rough recordings and burn them onto a compact disc.

When I moved out to Arizona, I didn't really know from the music scene back home. It wasn't until I began making visits back to San Francisco to see Dad that I became more aware. I had a childhood friend, Steve, who always seemed to be up on the latest trends. When I was in town, I would sometimes sleep over at Steve's, and he would play me tracks and albums from Bay Area rappers on his stereo. One that really stuck out to me was called *17 Reasons;* it was a compilation of local rappers who all had a distinct look and sound. On the cover a bunch of them were shown surrounding a tricked-out red '64 Impala parked on the Golden Gate Bridge. My first thought was, *Wow, these dudes are truly representing where I'm from.* I felt an instant connection to it. My second thought was, *I can't fucking* wait *to bring this shit back to Arizona and show this to all those fools who said that San Francisco was "soft."* The more I listened to that album, the more it spoke to me. I began researching the different rappers featured—like Andre Nickatina, Mac Dre, San Quinn, B-Legit, and Messy Marv—and in the process was awoken to just how vibrant and full the local rap community was. I'd listen to these dudes spit bars and think, *Damn, this is what I left behind when I moved to Arizona? I need to find a way to be a part of this.*

It was like the universe was looking out for me, because not long after, when I'd returned to Chandler, this dude came up to me outside of my school one afternoon and introduced himself as "Wicked Wizard."

"Are you a rapper?" he asked me. "You look like you could be a rapper."

OK, I thought, you've got my attention.

He asked if I knew how to freestyle. I told him I wasn't sure.

"Here," he said, "I'll show you." And he did a few lines of a freestyle rap and then told me it was my turn. I did my best and made a couple sentences rhyme. I'm sure it was awful. "Brother!" he said, "That shit was tight! You've gotta buy a machine and record some of that. Matter of fact, I have one in my car that I can sell to you." He pulled out a recording unit with two slots for a tape cassette from his trunk. "It's two hundred and fifty bucks," he said, "and you can plug in a microphone and record over beats and listen back. You put one tape with your beat into the left, then you record your vocals onto the tape in the left and *bam,* you've got a track. You seriously gotta pick this up."

"Really?" I didn't think my freestyle was that good.

"Oh, for sure. You're going to be famous, man. I can tell. You gotta have the tools to get you there!"

I went home, collected some of the cash I'd earned selling weed, and bought the machine, which was like an elevated version of a karaoke machine. (I know now that it was nothing close to what even a semiprofessional musician would be using.)

I thought Wicked Wizard truly believed in me. And then when I got to school and began telling some of my friends about it, I found out that a bunch of them had been given the same sales pitch. I'd been conned, but I didn't care. I used that machine all the time, practicing freestyles and rapping with my boys in Chandler. We'd pack into my garage in the insane Arizona heat, hotbox it, and fool around recording things. Then we'd head inside to my room where it was air-conditioned and listen to it. Hearing what was on the tape, I first realized that I might actually have some ability. My shit was sounding tight.

I had told Mom that I wanted to move back to San Francisco so I could explore the music scene and try to establish myself, and I did want that. But I quickly got swept up in the weed game and was filling most of my time between that, Tully's, and Jelly's. Music, it seemed, was relegated to the back burner.

But that all changed the day Don Toriano walked into Tully's during my shift.

Toriano was a rapper who was part of a group called Fully Loaded. He was an absolute local legend. He was a regular at Tully's—probably because we gave him free coffee milkshakes or whatever he wanted—and the place would be buzzing whenever he showed up. The first time I saw him there, one of my co-workers casually mentioned to him that I rapped. We started chatting, and Toriano began to take a liking to me. He brought me around to open mics, and we smoked tons of weed together. Between weed from Anthony, the Asians, and the Hemp Center, I always had some good bud on me, plus I could rap, so Toriano wanted to keep me around. As I hung out with them, I noticed that damn near all the rappers and musicians he introduced me to were smoking as well, and realized that weed and music tend to go hand in hand. Toriano brought me around to compete in rap battles, and I slowly started making a name for myself in the scene.

It was around this time that I met a fellow rapper named Stinje, who my longtime fans are very familiar with. To this day, Stinje is my best friend and my assistant and has appeared in many of my videos and other content, including the popular *Big Business* series on YouTube where he and I travel around the globe to meet fellow cannabis industry leaders. I was first introduced to Stinje by a co-worker at Tully's. Stinje is a tall, magnetic White guy who used to be able to rap better than me (ha). He had recording equipment at his apartment but no microphone; I had a microphone but no recording equipment. It was a match made in heaven. The first time I went to Stinje's place, I brought the microphone, and we ended up laying down four or five tracks on the spot. We recorded more than a hundred songs back in the day, amateur stuff, but we had a blast doing it. He gives me a hard time today because I've never released them—every time, I tell him that I never will.

Writing, rapping, and getting deeper into music was clutch for me. As busy as I was between my three jobs, the creative outlet that rap gave me was invaluable, and I began to devote myself more and more to music. Toriano hooked me up with a guy named Dunce, who was one of the biggest producers in San Francisco, and got me into a real recording studio for the first time, which conveniently was just a few blocks up the road from the coffee shop and around the corner from Stinje's place. Dunce produced all the Bay Area legends—including the artists from the *17 Reasons* compilation. He was super legit, and I know that when Toriano first brought me around to the studio, Dunce didn't take me seriously at all. In his eyes I was just this little kid who had good weed. But I knew I'd developed some skills, and I looked forward to proving him wrong.

Dunce and his team were using professional-grade music editing software called Pro Tools. But I had grown up recording on my shitty little karaoke machine, or with friends on a cheap four-track recorder. Using those things, you had to be able to get through your entire verse without making mistakes, because every time you screwed up, it meant going back to the very beginning of the track and starting all over again. And that was a major pain in the ass. So you had to be deliberate and on top of your game. With Pro Tools, on the other hand, you can go to any spot in a song and punch in vocals or edit, which meant that you could make a mistake and instead of re-recording the whole thing, you could just go back and fix the mistake. So I had learned how to record my verses in one take, which was a producer's dream, and this helped change Dunce's perception of me.

Every artist has their story, and this is mine. If you're reading this and you aspire to be a rapper, you can take a page out of my book. It wasn't magic. I just put in the work and the time. I learned about music and found a scene I knew I could be a part of. Over many years, I developed and curated my sound, which was inspired by the Bay Area rap vibe that had turned me on as a kid. I learned how to execute the craft and do it right and then made the connections with the people who could put me in a place to succeed. Point is: There are steps to success. You can't just jump in and do it. You're going to have to learn, and you're going to have to learn the hard way, which is often by failing. But that's how you learn. It wasn't long before I found my lane with the rappers, producers, members of the hip-hop community. Everything was coming together. As I added "rapper" I was throwing another log onto the fire.

. . .

For now, music was still only for my "free time," as I continued to hustle bar backing, barista-ing, and working at the Hemp Center for my 9–5. But my heart and mind were all in on the Hemp Center. Every day I spent there I felt like I was a part of something special, and I soaked in everything I could about cannabis and was absolutely falling in love with the communal nature of this plant and the way it brought people together. My first role was doing intake, and I saw it as a great responsibility to help create a welcoming, worthwhile experience for our patients. At intake, I was the first person a patient saw after entering the store. I created profiles for customers in our system and gave each one their patient number and called doctor's offices to confirm the validity of their medicinal marijuana card. Once they were in the system, all a patient had to do was give their patient number at the door, and their name would appear on my screen so I could greet them when they entered. Having customers logged in a database like this also let us track purchases so patients could find out which strains they had bought earlier, and it also enabled us to apply discounts and make notes about customers and their preferences. Some of the Hemp Center employees hated doing intake and signing up new customers, but I thoroughly enjoyed it. It was like I was able to be their gateway and guide into this wonderful world of weed. Kathleen, the Hemp Center owner, would observe me interacting with patients; she loved how I was naturally social with them and took the time to truly engage one-on-one. Within a month, she asked me to train to be a budtender (the person who works with patients to select the right strain for them and facilitate the transaction). I was a natural, and as much as I appreciated my role doing intake, budtending was where I truly began to shine. Being a good conversationalist, I hit it off with damn near every customer I served. They were so comfortable with me that sometimes I felt like I was a cab driver on an episode of *Taxicab Confessions*. I'd be weighing out their bud, and they would be spilling their hearts out about the latest drama happening in their life. It was just fun. The weed world in general was less regulated and more fun at that time. Nowadays, everything is prepackaged, but back then, all the products were displayed deli-style. The buds were out to be seen and touched and smelled and sampled. I'd hand-select good buds for patients, even give them small rips on a bong when new flavors arrived so they could sample it—kind of like how you'd taste-test flavors at the ice cream shop. Day after day, I was interacting with and studying a huge range of strains, and I felt I was truly making a positive difference in the well-being of our customers. Through the process of budtending, I was putting hundreds of hours of experience into showing people products, getting them excited, and turning it into a sale (it's easier said than done, but **these three skills alone—presenting a product, hyping it up, and closing the deal—will get you unbelievably far in business**). By the end of 2002, my first year at the Hemp Center, I felt I had mastered the art of selling.

I had also developed my first fan base—years before I ever released any music. My "fans" were my customers, and even if there were open registers available, they would line up and wait so they could deal with me specifically. Looking back, this was when I first began to discover my true personality and what made me stand out from the crowd. I realized that I was a likable guy and that people gravitated toward me, that there was something about my energy that people wanted to be around. I don't mean to sound cocky, but simply put, I realized that I had something special. Once I was able to identify that, it helped me understand my place in this world. I'm someone who brings the party together, who bridges gaps, and who makes people feel welcome, no matter what room I'm in. You'll hear me say this a lot, but as an entrepreneur it's so important to **never lose sight of the value you bring to the table.**

As I was settling in to my new life as a Hemp Center budtender, I arrived to work at Jelly's one night and found out that one of our bartenders had just been fired. "Junior," my dad's friend, the owner, called out to me as I entered the bar just before my shift began, "you're in tonight. And if anybody asks, you're twenty-one." In reality, I was only nineteen years old. But I learned fast. As a bartender, I was fast, paid attention to the details, and had a mouthpiece on me that made me a hit with the patrons. Before I knew it, I was budtending by day and bartending by night. Let me tell you, this was, by far, the greatest time of my life. There were women, weed, and money—and little responsibility. And all of it was fucking epic. The more life experiences I gained, the more my hunger for music grew; after all, now I had some wild shit to rap about.

For the next few years, I built up my rap game and was beginning to create some organic buzz. By 2005, I was still recording with Stinje and laying down tracks at Dunce's studio, where I was finding my pocket and learning how to write, record, mix, and arrange songs. I was also getting more comfortable with my own voice, which wasn't something that came automatically. My persona as a boss was being honed in the studio, and I felt I was ready to make a big move in music. The Hemp Center was proving to be an incredible networking tool; every person who passed through those doors could be another meaningful contact or connection. I had leveled up and become a buyer, looking at various products from vendors and deciding what the store should purchase—and at what price. One afternoon, a guy walked in with a diamond grill and comically huge chains on. "Hello, buddy!" he said, introducing himself as Haji Springer. Haji was a local Indian rapper who I later learned greeted *everyone* with "Hello, buddy!" He drove a Chrysler convertible that he had wrapped to look like a taxicab. We got to talking, and next thing I know I'm in the Chrysler smoking a joint with Haji as he plays me a CD with instrumental beats. Each one hit harder than the last. This was Dr. Dre–level production. I asked him where he got the beats from, figuring he must have downloaded them from some website. When he told me they were made by a nearby producer named Genesse, I instantly asked for an introduction. The wheels were starting to turn. I had a plan.

Around this time I had begun to form a connection with a Bay Area legend who went by Equipto. Just a few weeks before Haji turned me on to the Genesse beats, Equipto and I had talked about doing some sort of collaboration. I hadn't released a full professional album at this point and had been thinking long and hard about the best strategy for a debut release. My thought was, if I released a solo album out of the gate, nobody would care—at least not any sort of mainstream audience. But, if I released a collab album with someone already established—a legend in the game with an existing fan base that was large, cool, and knowledgeable—then audiences might take me more seriously. In retrospect, this was arguably my first marketing move. When Haji introduced me to Genesse, who agreed to produce beats for my album, the vision was complete. My plan was to package the best album possible and not only introduce myself as a new artist to Equipto's fans but also be known as the person who helped elevate the sound of a legend. In late 2006, Equipto and I hit the studio to record *Track Money and Pack Money,* and we were cooking from the jump. I knew the music would hold up. Then I designed eye-catching album artwork that featured me and a gorgeous woman in a pink short-skirt dress lying on a bed in a motel room. She's counting out giant wads of cash while I flip through the channels on the TV like it's just another Wednesday.

. . .

Even though I had, um, *embellished* about filming a documentary as a way to get my foot in the door at the Hemp Center, I still always had my video camera in tow and was constantly filming. I'd interview customers, bring the viewer behind the scenes of our operations, or simply position the camera at my register and leave it running all day. Now, whenever I got free time at nights, I'd edit the footage together the best I could, and post it online to WorldStarHipHop and YouTube, which were pretty new at the time. The videos started to go viral organically, and the Berner name was becoming more and more synonymous with the weed industry. At the same time, some of my rap albums were beginning to take off, and I was earning mad respect in the hip-hop community. Before I knew it, celebrities were showing up at the Hemp Center to smoke out with me, and I quickly started gaining access to more and more influential people.

One of the first celebs to hit me up was Wiz Khalifa.

Wiz came and we smoked big and became great friends from there. That relationship was genuine and illuminating. It gave me knowledge. And those videos I took with him got me popping. I was smart and documented all of it. I'd bust out my cellphone and make a video of us at the Hemp Center. Him coming into the store, trying the volcano bong, or smoking a fat-ass joint I rolled with some new strain called Cherry Pie—all of it I posted.

And so I became the celebrity weed guy.

Through Wiz I learned more about how the music industry worked, like which were the best studios and how I could get my foot in the door at iconic places like the Record Plant. In early 2007, *Track Money and Pack Money* was released, and I promoted it like it was my full-time job. I locked in a small distribution deal with a local business, City Hall Records, and formed my own label, Bern One Entertainment. I was able to take some of the money I earned selling weed and use it to buy billboards and put them up at places like Amoeba Music, Rasputin Music, and other California institutions to build up hype. In addition, I hired some local kids to put up thousands of flyers all over the Bay and posters up throughout San Francisco. The release made it look like I was getting the treatment of a label artist, even though I was still very much an indie artist. But I was able to fund it by myself thanks to my work ethic and the multiple roles I held, from buyer to dealer and now, finally, published artist.

The album was a big success and accomplished everything I'd wanted from it. It was such a hit that, if you look at my catalogue (I've recorded nearly forty-four albums by now), you'll notice I repeated the same playbook multiple times before dropping my first solo album, *Weekend at Bernie's*. My SOP (Standard Operating Procedure) was simple: Get great production from talented producers and engineers, find artists with an established and active fan base, record a collaboration album, package and promote it better than anything the artist had ever done before, and win over their fans. I was beginning to get a real understanding of the power of leverage and how to use the access I was getting—to exclusive weed, to influential artists, to people from all walks of life—to make anything possible.

. . .

I found the model in the pink dress on the cover of my debut album (the one lying on the bed counting all the cash while I was chilling nonchalantly) through a modeling agency. I went to go pick her up for the cover shoot, and she told me, "You know, my brother grows weed. You should meet him. His name is Mario."

Fuck it, why not?

Mario was growing weed out of the basement of his house in the Sunset District. He was Mexican Italian, just like me, with a thick goatee and elaborate tattoo sleeves covering each arm. He knew who I was through my work at the Hemp Center and the reputation I was building, both around the city and online, and wanted to get involved somehow. I went over to his crib to check out his operation and sample some of his weed. He was doing great work and cultivating a popular strain called Afghan, which tended to be a bit duller in smell, look, and flavor compared to the more exotic strains I liked to smoke. His weed wasn't going to turn any heads, but I dug his setup—he'd basically converted the entire basement and dedicated it to growing. Mario was cool, and he was eager to work with me. I took note; I knew he was somebody who I could fuck with and who brought value to the table.

At this time, just as I'd been making connections with musicians and elevating my game in the rap industry, I was forming close bonds with some innovative and influential dudes in the world of homegrown cannabis and had developed a group of friends—they would eventually become known as the "Cookies Fam"—who were experimenting with growing new genetics, which you can think of as the IP, or DNA, of marijuana strains. There were five of us: myself, Jai, Flux, Kenny Powerz, and now Mario.

Kenny Powerz is a guy who lived in the Sunset District. His brother was a very well-known legend from the Fillmore district named Shaka, who had been murdered. Shaka had been involved in all sorts of street shit, including breeding dogs and selling coke, which Kenny was also involved in. When I met Kenny around 2005, he was only selling weed, but back in the day he sold large amounts of cocaine as well. He told me he had had an epiphany while on a beach in Mexico and decided that he never wanted to deal coke again—he saw the damage it did to a growing number of addicts in his community—and was only going to sell weed going forward. Kenny used to always say, proudly, that he had transformed a cocaine block in Fillmore into a weed block. It became a hot spot in San Francisco, and famous smokers like rappers Method Man and Redman would come by Kenny's neighborhood to buy weed whenever they were in town. I first met Kenny in the early 2000s when I learned about his reputation. I rolled by his house to buy some weed for my own personal use, and it was bomb. It wasn't long before he was a regular at the Hemp Center. He'd come into the shop and open up a turkey bag full of his weed and show it off, which would piss Kathleen off because it wasn't weed that we carried. But Kenny would hold court and smoke and hang out with the staff and patients.

I first met Flux through Anthony. Flux, it turns out, was the guy who was supplying Anthony with his incredible weed from Humboldt. I used to sometimes roll with Anthony when he went to pick up from Flux, who lived in the Fillmore district at Fillmore and Haight Street. At the time Flux was known simply as Sean, and Anthony was always bragging about how his boy Sean had the *best* weed in California, including exclusive genetics that nobody else had. But it turned out that Flux and I went way back. I didn't connect the dots at first, but when I was a little kid in the third or fourth grade playing at Ray's house, Flux/Sean lived across the street and would come over to play with us sometimes. My primary memory of him back in those days is that he was a bully and would always flick the back of my ears. Fast forward to 2005, when I was a buyer at the Hemp Center. Flux walked in and said he was a vendor and had some awesome bud that we had to check out. One of my co-workers asked for his I.D. so we could put him into the system and he flipped. "My I.D.!?" he said. "Why, so you can know my address? Fuck that, I'm not giving you shit." The employee calmly explained that they couldn't do any business with him unless he provided his I.D. I was in the back room rolling a joint at the time and could hear the commotion through the door. Flux wrote his first and last name on a piece of paper and said that was all he was going to give before loudly proclaiming, "Fuck you, I'm out of here! This store only sells shit anyways." And he stormed out.

I finished rolling my J and went out to see what had happened. I took a look at the piece of paper and read the name "Sean Suarez."

Wouldn't it be funny, I thought, *if that was the same Sean Suarez who used to bully me back at Ray's house?* Flux had only made it a few steps down the block by the time I stepped out onto the sidewalk. "Hey, I'm a buyer here," I said. "What's going on?"

"That asshole inside is demanding my I.D., and I'm not going to give it to him." He was still heated.

I calmly said, "Look, bro, just come inside."

Back inside, cooler heads prevailed. He asked my name, and I said, "Gil, but I go by Berner." We chatted a bit longer, and he started to place my name. He asked if I was the same Gil who used to hang out with Ray and Anthony. I told him I was, and as we talked more I began to realize that this was the same Sean who Anthony had been boasting about getting his weed from. Anthony always had the best weed. Now, out of pure serendipity, the universe had hooked me up with my plug's plug. I didn't hesitate to buy from Flux, who became a Hemp Center vendor and first brought the strain Granddaddy Purple—one of the most popular in the game—to our store. He became known as the Purple Man, and he was making big deals with buyers out of state as well.

When I was working at Jelly's, I became friends with the owner's cousin, who introduced me to strip clubs and the nightlife scene. One night we were on our way to a local establishment, and he told me we should make a pit stop, he had to meet up with a guy who grew the best kush (a foundational strain) in the country. He made a call, and Jai pulled up. Jai is a soft-spoken dude who sported a long ponytail back in the day and had a calm, hippie-like energy. Jai was a purist, you could say, and wasn't as juiced about the business side of cannabis; Jai was all about the plant. His father was a Vietnam war vet and brought PTSD home with him, which I think made Jai's upbringing a bit difficult.

I bought an ounce from Jai right then and there. But when I bought the ounce, Jai also gave me an eighth of a different strain for free. He told me he was calling it Cherry Kush; it was a new type of strain that he was breeding from scratch. Jai was the first breeder I'd ever met. He was self-taught and learned by reading internet forums and through trial and error. You have to be a bit of a mad scientist to breed cannabis strains. It involves crossing the genetics, or DNA, of existing strains and balancing out the chemistry to create a brand-new strain—exactly the way two people can get together and have a child who shares genetics from both parents. The process is delicate: You take pollen from the male plant, transport it to a female plant, and produce a seed that is a cross of both plants. Jai was a gifted breeder who experimented at his house in the Sunset District.

When I smoked Jai's new strain, I was floored. It was *fire,* and I had never tried anything like it. At the time, the biggest strains were Trainwreck, Romulan, Northern Lights, Purple Kush, and Bubble Kush. But I'd never tried—or even heard of—Cherry Kush. Nobody had. It didn't get more exclusive than this. I got Jai's phone number and continued to buy from him. When I sold weed to my customers, I began to include very small amounts of Jai's Cherry Kush as well. I'd explain that it was some new stuff they'd never seen before, and people were very interested in getting their hands on more. It reminded me of when I was a kid in Arizona and first saw Anthony's weed and thought, *I need to get my hands on that.* I began to buy Cherry Kush by the pound and became the only dude in town selling it. It wasn't long before Jai was back in the lab and managed to somehow improve on the bud, breeding a new strain that I dubbed "Cherry Pie." It was the most popular weed I sold by far. The smell, bag appeal, and taste were so unique, and I was going viral online posting videos and other content showing off the Cherry Pie. Big rappers would come in from New York to buy it, and cannabis bloggers were coming by the Hemp Center and reporting on it as if we had discovered plutonium. As a weed plug, a friend, and eventually a partner, Jai gave me something that nobody else had, and that made me powerful.

While my status was rising at the Hemp Center, I was still dealing weed illegally to make extra cash on the side. I was still mainly selling Marvin's weed—the same Pineapple and Mango strains—and ended up buying some large quantities of the Granddaddy Purp from Flux for variety. Between my music career, climbing the ladder at the Hemp Center, and my weekend gig at Jelly's bar, I was wearing a ton of hats. But some days, it felt like my main hustle was my black market weed business. I'd leverage my position at the Hemp Center, and if I bought product from a vendor for the store, I'd also make a side deal with the vendor for my personal stash to sell off.

One day, I met a guy named Phil who was from Houston and said he wanted to buy off of me. "I want it all," he said. "Like, fifty pounds. Something like that." I thought he was nuts. I was dealing ounces and quarter pounds—maybe a pound, max. And this guy wanted fifty pounds!? My first thought was that this guy must be a fed. I started asking around, and another friend in town explained to me that he was no fed and was very legit and shopped big. "You should take him very seriously," the dealer said. "I'm getting old," he added. "You're young and hungry—fuck with him. Trust me." This became my introduction to the highly sketch world of out-of-state trafficking. I called up Phil and told him to stop by the Hemp Center and we'd work something out. He showed up the next day.

"You know," Phil said, "you're in the best position ever."

"How's that?" I asked.

"You sit in this store all day and buy weed. But you're not really being smart about it."

"Why not?"

"Well, you buy, let's say, a pound for the store or for yourself and you throw a couple extra dollars on it before you sell. Maybe a couple hundred bucks' profit. That's cute. But that's not real money." He handed me a JanSport backpack with $150,000 cash in it.

"I don't even know where to get that much weed," I said.

"What are you talking about? Look around. When vendors come in from now on, if they have Purple, Bubba Kush, or anything good, buy it for the store but also buy it for me."

A light bulb went off in my head. Now when a vendor came in,

I would say, "We'll take twenty-five pounds." I would keep maybe two pounds for the store, and the rest was for me to sell to Phil. The way I figured it, it was no harm; I was getting better pricing for the store while still getting my money elsewhere.

When Phil mentioned he wanted Granddaddy Purple, I immediately thought of Flux and began buying packs (one-pound bundles of weed) from him to resell to Phil. Phil ended up hooking me up with a buyer in Atlanta as well, so my side hustle enterprise was growing at an epic rate. I was making roughly $1,000 profit for every pound I sold, and the cash was piling up. I needed a safe place to store it—I ended up stashing it in a spare room I rented out in my sister's apartment. I was mad paranoid operating in the black market. I would never meet people near the apartment; instead I would arrange meetings at a local laundromat. I'd fill a huge duffel bag with weed and carry along a giant Costco-sized bottle of Tide laundry detergent so I didn't look suspicious. You always had to be on the lookout for authorities or thieves and other shady characters. In the medical market, there was at least some form of protection. We had a door with a lock on it at the dispensary, and Prop 215 offered vague legal protections. But out on the streets? I felt totally exposed, as if I were carrying all the risk in the world.

. . .

Before long, my crew—Jai, Flux, Kenny, Mario, and myself—was producing some of the most hype genetics around. The crew worked well together, at first. We each brought something to the table. Jai was the first one in the group to begin breeding and experimenting; Flux was a seasoned hustler and an influential broker who moved a lot of weight, both on the streets and in the medical market; Kenny supplied the original marijuana plant, called F1 Durban, that was used to breed with another strain, OG Kush, to create Girl Scout Cookies; Mario opened his home to the crew to carry out breeding projects and, aside from hosting us, brought one of the parent plants that was used to create the Gelato and Sunset Sherbet strains, which remain two of the most popular strains to this day; they are absolute cornerstones of the global cannabis market. As for myself, I brought the hype, and I was the most comfortable of us in any kind of setting. People have been telling me my whole life that I have a light around me when I walk into a room. I had the rapping going and a legit fan base on social media. I had a ton of buzz at the time in both the white market (licensed dispensaries) and the black market (the streets), and I could take their work and make it something special. I even created Instagram accounts for each member of the crew and built up their followings using my own fan base, which today is at two million (and would be way higher if Instagram and other platforms didn't restrict so much of the weed-based content I post). Put it this way: A lot of people can create and breed cannabis, but not a lot of people can popularize it. It's like how traditionally a musician needs the backing of a record label to help produce, market, and spread their art to the masses. I looked at myself like the label. Just like I'd brought that Cali weed to Arizona back when I was a kid, I knew how to get the right product in the hands of the right people. I knew how to hustle, and I knew how to brand it.

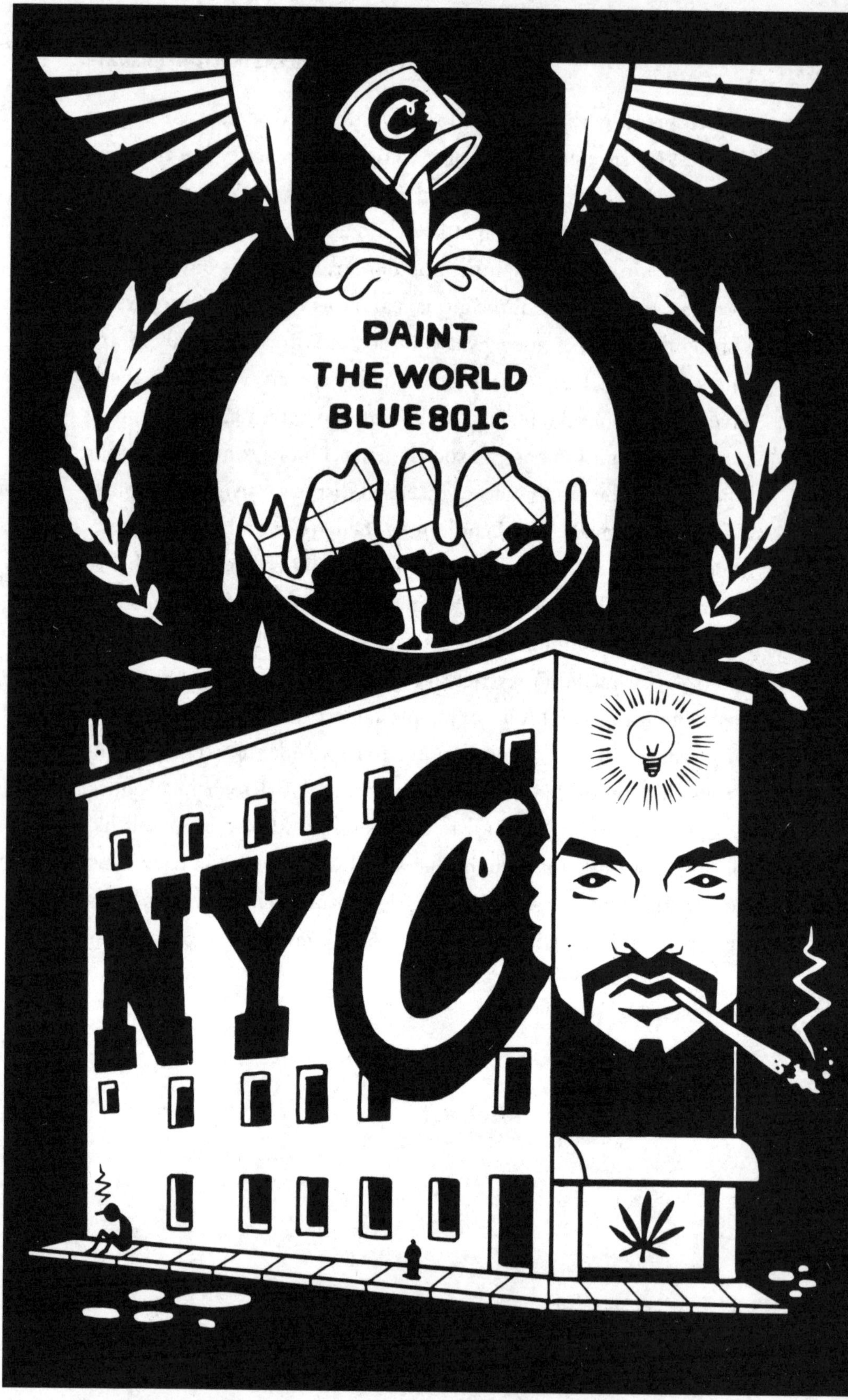
PAINT
THE WORLD
BLUE 801c
NY

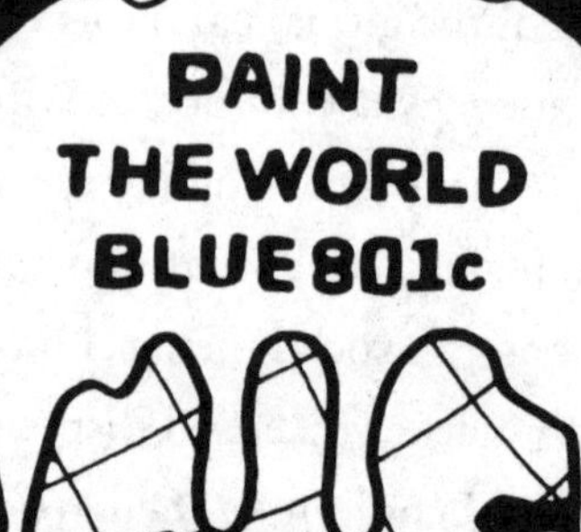

Chapter 4

MAKE YOUR IDENTITY TIMELESS: PAINT THE WORLD BLUE

There are a few ingredients I consider absolutely necessary when it comes to building a recognized, timeless brand. You need a catchy name—something that sounds familiar anywhere in the world. You need a standout logo, one that's clean and legible that you can stamp on just about anything. You need a unique colorway that defines the character of your brand. And you need a founder with vision and an authentic story that people can get behind to put a face—and soul—to your business. Most importantly, you need to be extremely passionate about what it is you're building; without passion, your business will never truly resonate with consumers.

There it is. That's the formula.

Take these qualities and attach them to a great product, and I promise your brand will have a shot. That is how I turned Cookies into a household name, and even today it's how I'm putting newer brands like Lemonnade and Vibes on the map. Developing, establishing, and sustaining a brand is a nonstop grind, and branding is at the heart of nearly every decision I make. I'm still trying to paint the world blue.

. . .

In the birth and life of any business, there are moments—monumental, life-altering moments—that set you on a path to greatness. You'll remember these moments like you remember the birth of your kids. The day I first tried Girl Scout Cookies, which would become arguably the most popular product I've ever been associated with, was definitely one of those moments.

It was the spring of 2008, and I had a day off from my gig at the Hemp Center and was working on some tracks in the janky home studio I'd built in the garage of my house on 41st and Noriega. With all the hats I was wearing between the budtending, getting my rap career off the ground, the trials and errors of a clothing line I was dreaming of, and the network of grows the crew and I were developing, the grind truly never stopped. Still, I was always coming up with ideas for new businesses.

Frustrated that I could never find any good clothes sized 2XL or larger, my mind drifted from editing tracks as I thought about starting a plus-size men's clothing line. *I'll call it: Presidential.* The thought was interrupted by a knock at the garage door.

I slid the metal frame up about halfway and Jai ducked under and into the makeshift studio. Inside the garage was a door leading to a laundry room where I kept my scale and would check out the herb that people had dropped off. Jai made a beeline to the laundry room. He had the biggest smile on his face. His backpack smelled like an entire grow room as he passed by me. *The fuck is in that bag?* I wondered.

When we got to the laundry room, he pulled out a turkey bag with a pound of sticky, funky buds tinted dark blue like the ocean (which was just a few blocks away). When I opened the bag, the whole pound was all stuck together in the shape of a football. I broke down a few buds with my fingers as the pungent aroma of dank herb filled the room.

"You smell her?" Jai began, hyping it up. "You feel how sticky she is? Get in on that."

I split open a Swisher blunt and rolled one. I set it on the windowsill and let the sun hit it real quick, to give it a graham cracker texture that burned smooth.

"It taste wild, B," Jai kept going. "Trust me." The guy was juiced.

After a few minutes, I fired it up.

"Smell that in the air? Let it coat your palate."

I took a hit and had never tasted anything like it. It checked all the boxes: sweet but gassy, leaving a soapy smell in the air and a lingering taste in my mouth that reminded me of something specific. Something I couldn't exactly put my finger on . . .

"What *is* that, J?" I asked.

"It's that thin mint," he said. "She taste like a Girl Scout cookie."

Girl Scout Cookies!? I may have been stoned, but I wasn't trippin'. I knew instantly it was the perfect name.

A few months earlier I had come up with the name Cherry Pie for another one of our strains, which became a huge success among medical cannabis users and an even bigger hit on the underground market. So this felt like a natural follow-up. I started sharing Girl Scout Cookies with a very limited set of customers on the streets. I also gave it to influential rappers and producers like Snoop Dogg, Rick Ross, Currency, Wiz Khalifa, Chris

Brown, and Alchemist—they would get a quarter ounce to smoke and hype up. Soon, I was buying a pound off Jai and selling it for $4,800 to people in New York City and across the country. It went from extremely limited to available everywhere, and I became this mythical trapper overnight—going from the guy known for giving rappers exclusive weed and talking about it in my music and online to the person who was putting the weed everywhere around the world.

Except I wasn't. I was still limited with who I was selling to, but the knockoff genetics were popping up all over the place. People were selling leaks—basically their own version of Girl Scout Cookies—and calling it "Berner's Cookies" and crediting me with spreading it to the masses. If some dude was selling fake cookies in Memphis, he told people it came from Berner. I heard so many stories of local dealers bragging about "I got a direct line to Berner, we're close like that, this shit came straight from him." It was all lies, and it was happening all over the country. It was wild, but it was all building my name, just like stories would be passed around that William Wallace killed a thousand men and this and that. All of that helped his legend grow. The misconception ended up helping to build the hype for myself and the product. Girl Scout Cookies hit the streets and appeared in dispensaries and took off and became one of the most sought-after genetics in the world. Sunset Sherbet, Gelato, and other foundational genetics that remain in the DNA of today's bestselling cannabis strains followed.

Our profiles were growing fast. I'll never forget when we all pulled up to the *High Times* Cannabis Cup—an annual celebration of weed—in Richmond, California, in 2013. Crowds gathered around us instantly from the buzz coming off our genetics, and it was so cool to see that sort of following and attention from within that community. We were mixing with the people and feeling like baby celebrities from the weed we were putting out. It was a great feeling.

People were willing to pay tens of thousands of dollars just for a leaked cut of our genetics, and the Cookies Fam was changing the flavor profile for cannabis consumers around the world. The dessert lane was officially ours. Looking back, the timing was perfect. It was the birth of social media. There was no censorship online, and I could post pictures and videos of weed—which you can't do anymore. I owned that world.

. . .

With all the hype in the industry and a growing staple of proprietary genetics, we needed a brand, an identity that could be applied to more than just one strain. Even though legalization still seemed a long way away, I wanted to approach the cannabis business like any other. From the moment I first stepped into the Hemp Center and began my education in the world of legal weed, I knew that once cannabis became regulated for recreational use, the first real brand in the space would win. At the time, there was no branding in the space at all, and I was determined to change that. To become that first real brand.

At the Hemp Center, I was getting a legit education in marketing and branding herb. As buyers, it was always up to us to merchandise and sell product. Someone would come in with a batch to sell me, and the grower had usually named the strain. "This is called California Orange, or Cali O," a vendor would say. I'd pay for the weed, which usually came in an unlabeled bag, and put it in a display jar on the shelf. In front of the jar we'd place postcards with the name of the weed and the price written on it. The other budtenders would simply write:

"Cali O"
8th—$50
Quarter—$100
Half-oz—$150
Zip—$300

But I would take that postcard and make an orange font, with a clean-ass "O" and a wavy creative background using some colored pencil crayons that were lying around. I'm no graphic artist, but I used to do some tagging, and I enjoyed messing around trying different fonts. I was just vibing, high and a little bored. But I still wanted to make it look tight. I figured: The weed was bomb, and I wanted to represent it right. So when people came up to the shelf they'd see these plain signs and then super-exciting ones, and they'd ask, "What's *that* one?"

It didn't take long for me to realize, *Damn, the more detail you put into signage, the more people are going to pay attention.* I didn't know it at the time, but this was my introduction to the power of branding. It was like someone had turned my light on.

I really got into the postcards. Vendors would bring in herb, and my first thought was how I would design the product card. Soon the other budtenders got into it, too. Some dude would bring in Super Skunk, and I'd yell, "Hey, can anyone draw a skunk?" And customers were really gravitating to it. There were times I felt like the Hemp Center's art director. Someone could have looked at the whole scene and said, "Whatever, he's making a fucking sign for the weed—*big deal.*" But I was beginning to see the bigger picture.

Still, branding in cannabis was almost an oxymoron back then. At the time it was such a low-key business. Not legal, not illegal, in this gray area. People in the industry were just thinking about survival, like, "Let's get this weed harvested safely, get it sold, and get our money back." That was the attitude back then. "Let's sell some weed." End of conversation.

But pretty soon vendors noticed what we were doing. They'd notice that the "Cali O" in the orange font was selling faster than the other strains. I would get rewarded by vendors who saw how our creative signs were not only helping to move their product faster but were putting some sort of respect on it, too. They'd hook me up with free ounces and other perks. It was a win-win, and I was having a blast doing it.

Apart from the product cards, I paid close attention when we began carrying products from a company called Tainted. While other companies put their edibles in a clear plastic wrap, Tainted made chocolate edibles in a package that resembled brand-name candy bars, like Snickers or Reese's. They were marketed to stoners, and looked just like the real thing. People would talk about it. I saw so many people come in, have a chuckle, and buy a dozen Reese's cups saying they wanted to hand them out to their friends. "Damn," I thought, "you don't even know if this shit is any good or not?" Eventually, that company got sued, which I guess was inevitable. But the lesson stuck: Branding matters.

. . .

With a product people loved in the Girl Scout Cookies strain, a growing online fan base, and a vision for multiple product lines under one canopy, it was time to create our look and feel. But first we needed a name. I looked at the successful brands out there. Are they easy to say out loud? Do they feel welcoming? Are they instantly recognizable? I thought about one-word brands like Nike and Adidas. Think of how familiar those are to us all; there is so much power in those single words. I wanted my brand to have the same impact. A good brand name flows off the tongue, like people have been talking about it long before it ever existed. And if you want to take what you're building around the world, then you need a name, or word, that all people recognize. For example: *Love*.

I knew it was important to tie into the success of Girl Scout Cookies, which was being bootlegged all over the place. When Jai was still growing it in an uncontrolled environment in his basement, some of the batches would come out with seeds in the bag alongside the harvested buds. Because it was his only grow at the time, he'd sell the seeded packs anyway, which people don't usually want. But I'm a great marketer, so we created the campaign "If it ain't got the seed, it ain't got the breed." It made the seeded bags feel "limited," "exotic," "unique." And it worked. People were hype to buy them. But as a result, Girl Scout Cookies ended up appearing *everywhere*. Other companies began growing their own versions using our seeds, and I first began to consider the concept of licensing marijuana. The crew, on the other hand, thought we were getting fucked over, but I learned to view it as a positive that competitors were promoting our product and spreading our name for free. You can't buy that kind of exposure. (One of the most common questions we would get was "Is this the *real* Girl Scout Cookies?")

To this day, we're one of the more bootlegged brands around. As with counterfeit Gucci handbags, Homeland Security regularly seizes entire shipments of bootlegged vape pens or lighters with our branding on them.

Bootlegging can be the biggest form of flattery, but it'll also affect your business. As much hype as the name *Girl Scout Cookies* had, I knew we had to avoid pissing off the Girl Scouts of America. So eventually I decided to just go with *Cookies*. But yes, we did get a cease-and-desist letter from Girl Scouts of America before that.

As soon as I said it aloud, not only did I think it was dope, but I knew exactly what it was. I could picture it all. The clothing. The herb. The multiple SKUs. The mass appeal. Guess what exists in every country? Go to China, Mexico, anywhere, and the word *cookies* will elicit a response. I could have named my shit something like "Zeratek." But is "Zeratek" ever going to be a tight-ass, respected streetwear brand? Probably not. But I knew Cookies could be.

Once we had a name, it was time to design the logo, which I thought should be a script of the word *Cookies*. Simple. Classic. Unmistakable. It had been about a year since we developed the concept of creating a brand, and to bring the idea to life we needed a font that was bold, but friendly, loud but familiar. I knew just the man to call.

Most people knew Shemp as "Photo Doctor." He was the most popular illustrator in the Bay Area when it came to designing hip-hop album covers. He was a talented dude who had a gift for taking existing fonts and redesigning or customizing elements to make them his own. He had a sharp eye for detail and had done all my albums. He also did the album covers for most all the Bay Area rappers I looked up to, like Mac Dre and Messy Marv. If you were putting together a project, Shemp was the guy you wanted to reach out to. So I hit him up and explained to him what I needed. "Something welcoming and familiar," I said. "Something that's going to stick." It was a work-for-hire situation, and I paid him something like $1,000 for his time and effort. A few days later he showed me the Cookies wordmark that you know today. We never had a contract or any sort of written agreement, but I still work closely with Shemp to this day and recently gave him $25,000 out of respect and as a gesture of good faith. I know you might look at that number and think it sounds low, but work for hire is work for hire.

Legend has it that the designer of the original Twitter logo got paid $15, and that the designer of the Nike logo was paid just $35. Shemp and I had a great talk and arrived at a figure that was fair and left him taken care of.

Next, I needed to select the color. I wanted one universal colorway to use across my brand. I cannot emphasize how crucial this is to your identity. Keep things consistent, whether it's packaging, clothing, exit bags, anything. At the time, the San Francisco streetwear brand Diamond Supply had an exclusive run of Tiffany-colored exit bags that were in high demand, and they were the inspiration for the blue color I eventually chose. Diamond Supply had landed on my radar via Wiz Khalifa and some other artists I was hanging around, who would receive these care packages from Diamond Supply. Shemp and I were in the garage, flipping through a Pantone book looking for a similar blue that spoke to us. And there it was: 801 C, a shade of neon blue. It just *popped.* When I first saw that blue script on a black background, I knew we had our logo. It was powerful and unique. The logo felt like something that belonged in the world. Something with staying power.

Today, I watch people leave my stores with those 801 C blue exit bags, and I can't help but smile. They just scream "Cookies." In states where there are regulations over the way cannabis brands and signage can exist in their markets, like New York or Arkansas, that sky-blue building is enough for people to know it's a Cookies-related store. From buildings to clothing to packaging, that blue has helped establish Cookies as an extremely clean, consistent, recognizable brand.

With a logo and colorway selected, we still needed an icon. The bitten apple from Apple, the Swoosh from Nike, or the Jumpman from Jordan.

I was smoking a four-gram joint at the Hemp Center one afternoon and brainstorming ideas when an animated motherfucker with bug eyes who looked like Earthworm Jim walked in. He had a black notebook in one hand and a backpack slung over one shoulder. He introduced himself as Al Freshko. I recognized the name as the guy who had designed the logo for Diamond Supply, as well as logos for the skate company Chocolate and several other iconic Bay Area brands. Al was a character. He would slip into funny voices and was always cracking jokes. I liked him instantly. He was cocky and confident and kept referring to his "steez," which is another word for style.

We started talking about Cookies, and Al asked what I was planning for the logo. I was already sold on his energy and knew right away that I needed to have him design it. I broke down some exotic, exclusive bud and rolled one for him. "Pull out your pencils," I said.

I grabbed a pencil and a piece of scrap paper and began to draw a big circle with a bite taken out of it. A lot of my designs start out with the shadiest little unimpressive doodles. And this one did, too. In the middle of the circle I added the ugliest C inside of it. Al smiled as he started to get what I was envisioning. He pulled a portable speaker out of his backpack and put on some jazz. Al was in the zone. He turned to a blank page in his notebook and began re-creating my shady mock-up. The dispensary had filled up with smoke by now, and a small audience of staff and customers had gathered around Al. Everyone was vibing and watching Al work his magic. It felt like some real underground shit. He took a picture of the sketch with his iPhone and transferred the image to his computer, where he was able to put the finishing touches on digitally. After a few minutes he turned that computer screen around and showed me the finished icon. To see that sketch I'd handed him come to life like that was a high of its own. We added the

801 C Pantone blue to the icon, and it was game over. Al started showing me the different ways we could use the icon, and it opened my eyes to what I actually held in my hands: I had global recognition, a huge online following, some of the world's best cannabis genetics, and now, a brand—Cookies—to bring it all together.

If only it was that easy.

How can you trademark the word *Cookies*? It's a question that has kept me awake at night. Despite being amped up at how the brand identity had come together, I still had some serious hurdles in my way. And, like any entrepreneur trying to get a brand off the ground, I had to get creative.

. . .

"Yo, B, turn on the TV!" It was Thanksgiving Day a few years back, and the famous Macy's Thanksgiving Day Parade was under way in New York City, where I knew some of my partners were enjoying the view from the rooftop of one of our largest Cookies stores yet. They were chilling on the roof, smoking and sending pictures of the balloons passing by. I flipped on the television just in time to see the camera pan across the street and reveal that distinct blue building prominently in the background. It's five stories and right across the street from Macy's, so you can't miss it.

You can drive down Melrose Avenue in Hollywood, or watch the Thanksgiving Day parade on TV and no matter where you are, you see that Cookies blue and you know it's me. *That's* the power of good branding. You can be somewhere in Asia or Central America, and you see someone wearing a Cookies hat, and there's an instant unspoken bond, like our logo is some sort of international smoke signal that draws people together.

That is what an effective brand can accomplish. Your identity is everything, and it's a corner you should never cut. Your brand is your personality. It's your drive. It's your way of life. Feelings, memories . . . all of it is wrapped up in your brand.

Develop a strong brand, and you'll have a chance to paint the world in your colors, too.

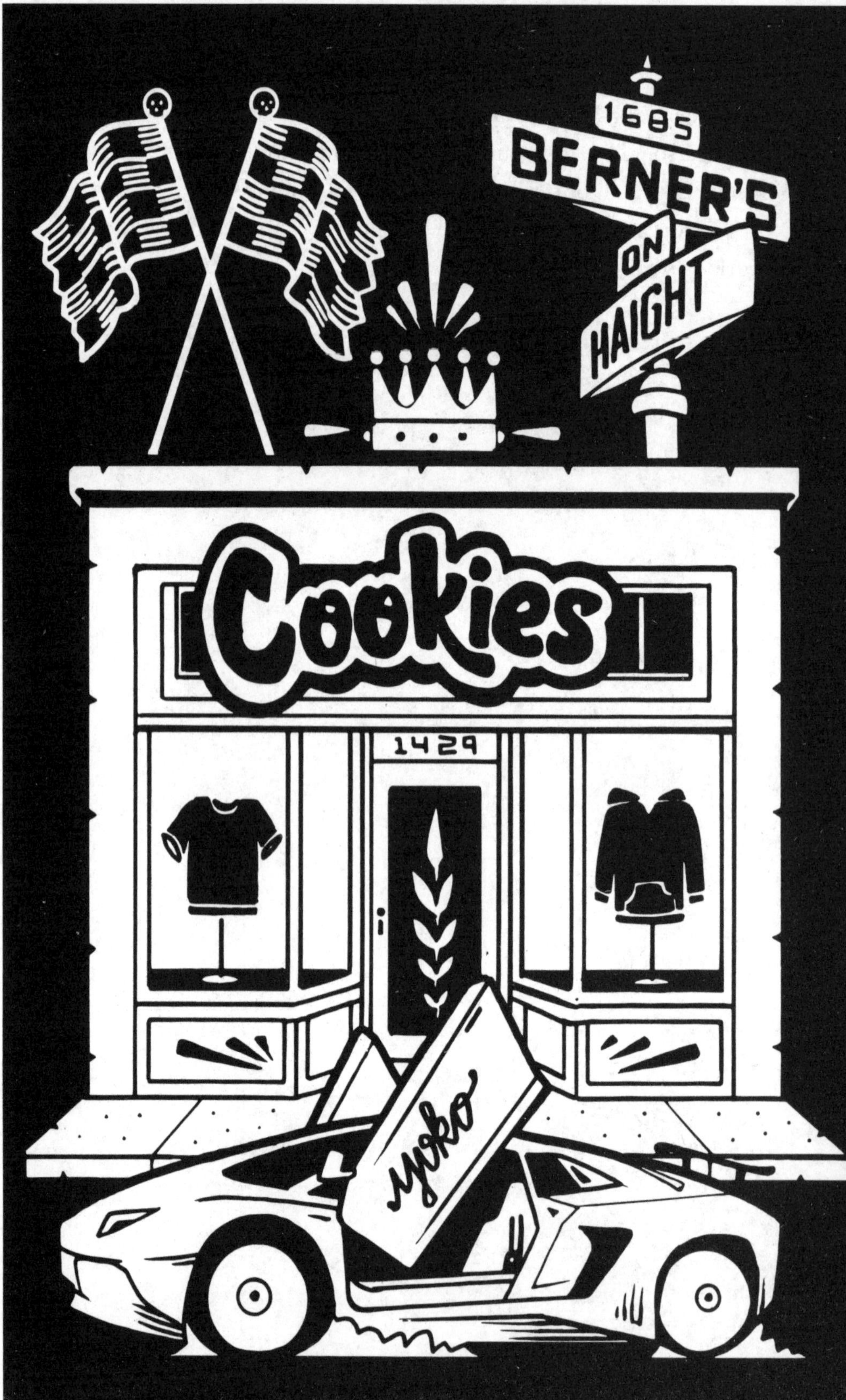
1685
BERNER'S
ON
HAIGHT
Cookies
1429
yoko

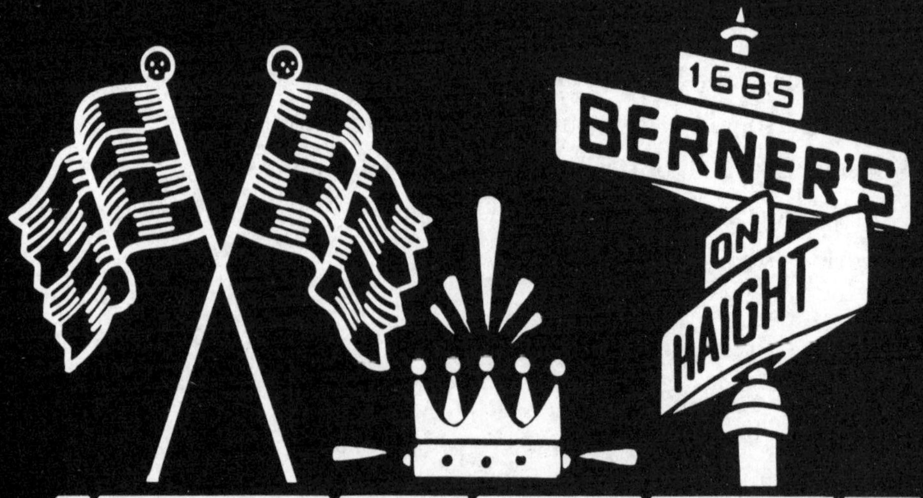

Chapter 5

"NO" IS CODE FOR "NEGOTIATE"

At the end of the day, building a successful business is about getting to a "yes"—whether you're negotiating with potential business partners or with yourself. But it's hard to get people to change their mind, and it can be even harder to change yourself. You need to know what motivates the person across the table from you—or the person looking back at you in the mirror—and sometimes you need to convince yourself to take a risk that seems crazy or change course even when that course has been paying the bills. I've always been comfortable in the uncomfortable place of hearing "no." And you need to be, too. Because to be a true whale you have to understand that a "no" is simply the first step in a negotiation.

. . .

As hard as it might be for some, many people like saying the word "no." It's a subconscious thing, a neurological reaction in your brain. Saying "no" to someone can make you feel empowered or protected. "Yes," on the other hand, leaves you vulnerable. "Yes" can be risky; "no" is safe. It's one of the reasons you can expect to hear "no" a lot on your journey to the top. I sure as shit did. But if you want to succeed, you have to be able to look at that "no" as the threat it is and be prepared to fight to get a "yes." That mindset is the foundation of effective negotiating. "No" has never stopped me before. It has barely slowed me down.

When it comes to perfecting my negotiating skills, I have to give my mom credit. She had just about the coldest mouthpiece I've ever seen, and the thousands of hours I overheard her wielding that shit like a weapon clearly made an impression on me. When we moved to Arizona, Mom started her own business as a headhunter, working out of our place in Chandler. Once you took a step through the front door, directly to the left was the living room, where she set up her desk and created a home office. To the right of the entrance, at the front of the house, was my bedroom. I can't tell you how many times I heard her working her magic. I'd be in my room, chilling, on some daydreaming shit. Through the paper-thin pine bedroom door I could hear her laugh and her smooth, positive approach with whoever was on the other line, all day long. Mom's job was to find a person who met particular criteria and get them to leave their job and, in some cases, to relocate their whole family for a job opportunity at a new company. As you can imagine, she heard "no" a lot more than she heard "yes." But she was never discouraged—if she was, she hid it well—and had a way of winning people over. On the phone, Mom was incredibly personable. She made people feel comfortable, joked around, and made sure to find common ground. She'd present them with the opportunity early in the conversation and then pivot to find some sort of personal connection until she could win them over with her personality. Once they were comfortable and a relationship had been formed, then she would circle back to the opportunity, after having built up personal equity with the person she was convincing to uproot their life. She was great at it. Her interpersonal skills and ability to connect with people through conversation were eye-opening to me. And as much as she'd kill 'em with kindness, Mom knew how to turn up the heat when she needed to.

I remember one September afternoon, I was chilling in my room, listening to Nirvana's *Unplugged in New York* album. I was sixteen years old, and we had recently moved back to San Francisco to a house in the Sunset District. I sat on my bed, closed my eyes, and thought about what life must have been like for Kurt Cobain and the band. Traveling from city to city, life on the road, the rock-star lifestyle. I thought it was the coolest shit in the world. *I should be out there,* I thought, *on the road, seeing the world.* I pictured myself as Cobain's homie and imagined that I might have been able to stop him from killing himself. Then I heard Mom's voice from her home office, saying firmly but not shouting: "You're discriminating against my sons."

I snapped out of my daydream. Mom had moved us into the neighborhood purposefully so my brother and I could go to Lincoln, a high school a few blocks away with a good reputation. "This is ridiculous. We live four blocks away." The school board had denied our admission and were trying to send us to Mission High, which was way out of the way and just a bad environment for me with a lot more traps to get into trouble. "I hear you," she told the person on the other line, who I later learned was the principal at Lincoln. "I hear that you don't have much space there and are trying to redirect them to another school. I understand. But, as I said, I feel like you are discriminating." I was hanging on every word.

"If we don't make it happen," she continued, "then I'm going to feel the need to go directly to the school board with this. And that's going to cause big problems." There was a pause, and then Mom calmly said: "You have to understand that I'm not going to stop until we figure this out."

I'll never forget her tone. Cool and collected, stern but respectful the whole time. When the school told her "no," she put her foot down. She raised hell. And she did it with class. She wasn't being nasty, yelling and hanging up the phone in rage. She stayed respectful—but never wavered from her end goal. Ultimately, she got what she wanted. The next day we started our first day at Lincoln High. I may not have known it at the time, but I soaked up lots of game from Mom, and I am forever grateful for that.

. . .

Turning negatives into positives is a guiding principle that's served me well. I don't let roadblocks get in my way. Often that means finding creative ways to make the most of "opportunities" that may look at first like dead ends. I'm sure you experience moments like this all the time, too. Whether you asked out the girl or guy you've been crushing on and got rejected or are trying to get into a club and the bouncer tells you it's full, whatever the obstacle, it's on you to do what it takes to get on the ladder and begin climbing.

I think about the way I got my first job. At the time I was doing whatever I could to get my foot in the door. But looking back, I was getting early reps in how to negotiate. I was thirteen or fourteen years old, and I saw that Oscar's, an Italian restaurant next door to the movie theater my friends and I hung out at, was hiring. I asked how old you had to be to work there, and they told me fifteen. Cool, I said, no problem. I came back the next day, said I was fifteen, and applied for the job. I told them I'd work my ass off—and

I meant it. They gave me a shot. At first they had me handing out breadsticks in front of the movie theater, trying to attract people into the restaurant. That was amazing. I mean, sure, all my friends saw me there and laughed at me, but it helped me get comfortable pitching to strangers. And I was naturally good at it. After about a week they had me bussing tables, and I was crushing it. I made a lot of tips as a busboy, which isn't typical. A few weeks later, I was named Employee of the Month. That was right around the time they realized I wasn't fifteen and had to let me go. I hated not having control over that decision, but I'd proven to myself that I could talk and act my way through doors that were seemingly sealed shut, because the lock could be jimmied if you just went about it the right way.

. . .

I have already mentioned that, from a bird's-eye view, my origin story may look messy, with so much happening all at once, and that was true even when I was starting to map out and build Cookies.

In 2009, at the age of twenty-five, I landed at SFO airport in San Francisco after a recent trip to Atlanta, where I was working on my music as well as moving through some weight—at that time it would have been the strains Granddaddy Purple and OG Kush, and there was a surprise waiting for me at the baggage claim—the Drug Enforcement Administration.

"You got a second?" asked a man in a plain white T-shirt and jeans. He was wearing a black hat with curly blond hair poking out of the sides. He approached me as I walked off the airplane on my way to collect my baggage. I thought he recognized me from my social media and wanted a picture. Low-key, I was poppin'. Nope.

Turns out, he wanted to search my bag, count any money I had on me, and ask me a ton of questions about my trip and my crew, and he wanted to do it right there in the middle of the airport. I knew the drill; this shit was nothing new to me.

I'd been questioned and harassed by the authorities since I first started working at the Hemp Center and started documenting my journey on social media. Throw in the multiple trips I was taking to places like Jamaica and Amsterdam, where I represented the Hemp Center as a judge at the Cannabis Cup awards, and I had gotten used to being a target for the DEA. To this day, I refuse to fly into LAX because I have post-traumatic stress disorder from the number of times I was pulled aside by DEA and harassed. I used to think it was all part of the game. Hell, I almost *liked* the attention. But life was moving fast, and my world was changing. I was married to my first wife, Sophia, who had two children I was helping to raise, and our daughter, Janelle, was just getting out of diapers. There's nothing that will change your perspective like having a child. That shit hit differently now. Life, hustling, the DEA . . . all of it.

Frustrated, I ignored the agent's questions—it's not like I was being arrested—and got my bag and headed outside the terminal and popped a seat on the curb while I waited for my family to pick me up. A few moments later, my wife's car pulled up curbside, but she was riding solo, which was extremely strange.

"Where the kids at?" I asked her.

"They're at your mother's," she told me.

When we arrived at Mom's house, the kids weren't there. Instead, my mom, Matt, and our cousin Tina were all sitting on the living room couch. On a table in front of them was a bottle of champagne on ice.

"Sit down, baby," Mom told me. That's when I noticed the tears dripping down Sophia's cheeks.

Mom began to explain that she had Stage 4 stomach cancer and how she was determined to fight but was worried she didn't have much time left. I was in shock. Frozen. I couldn't even tear up. My mom had always been my hero and my best friend. She was the only person I could trust to raise Janelle if anything ever happened to me. As she spoke, I couldn't comprehend the words. They didn't make any sense. She looked so strong and healthy.

For a long time, I was in denial. I didn't want to believe it. At first removing her stomach was an option and, if things went right, she would possibly have another ten years to live. But her battle turned into a roller-coaster ride in a hurry. When they went to put a chemotherapy port in her chest, they punctured a main vein, causing a massive blood clot, which essentially took chemo completely off the table. Instead, doctors told her there was basically nothing they could do. It felt like mistake after mistake was being made by Kaiser Permanente, which was in charge of her treatment, and I just remember thinking how unfair it all felt for Mom.

Over the next few months her condition deteriorated. Badly. While I was caring for Mom, I put my weed hustle on pause. How was I supposed to think about my out-of-town customers while draining fluid from her lungs or changing her diapers or, at the very end, rubbing ice chips on her lips in the hopes that it would hydrate her? I was forced to connect Flux, who I'd been buying from in bulk to sell to Phil in Houston, directly with Phil. They knew what I was going through, and they had promised to put a few points on each end aside for me so that I could help Mom with her battle while still earning. That meant that I was supposed to get $200 from Flux for every pound he sold, and $200 from Phil for every pound he bought, which would have worked out to $400 per pound for me. They honored our agreement—only once—and then fucked me royally. Around the same time, the stash of cash I kept in my new apartment was robbed, and I lost $170,000 in the blink of an eye.

Mom was losing her battle quickly. She was on her deathbed. Extended family members came by the house to say their goodbyes, and a priest came in to read her her last rites. Mom had two dogs, Labrador retrievers that she loved, and one of my uncles was making plans to put them down after her death. But there was one doctor at a local hospital, an older Chinese man, who said he had a solution that wouldn't extend her life but would at least make her more comfortable. "What's up?" I asked. He said he had a plan to cut her open by her lungs, put a tube in, and drain the fluid so she could breathe better. One of Mom's brothers had the final word on whether to pull the plug or not, and he said he didn't want to go ahead with the procedure, because everybody had already said their goodbyes to Mom. "It's time to let her go," my uncle said.

"No, it's fucking not," I replied. "If you let her go I'm going to smash your face open. Let the doctor do his thing."

I was intimidating when I had to be, and my uncle allowed it to happen. When the doctor did the procedure, it was like a scene straight out of a movie. He drained the fluid, and she woke right up, completely alert. "Oh my god," she said. "What happened?"

"Dude, they were going to let you go!" I told her. "They were planning to put down the dogs!" Enraged, Mom grabbed a pen and a piece of paper and wrote out instructions: *Let my dogs live for the rest of their natural lives, and my son Gilbert has the final say on what happens to me from now on.*

A couple of weeks later, Mom was out of the hospital. She enjoyed Thanksgiving, Christmas, and New Year's with us, and then died on January 16th. It had been seven months since she first told us she was sick. When she died, I was numb. On top of the grief I was feeling, I was being burned in the game, catching heat from the DEA, and watching friends of mine get locked up. I needed to figure things out and make some changes.

In 2009, while Cookies, the brand, was still mostly an idea percolating in the back of my mind and I was still a few months away from sitting with Shemp and creating our logo, I thought one possible way forward was to start a clothing company. I had seen the impact that Diamond Supply was having in the streetwear scene, and I thought I could get my clothing company off the ground. I tried my best with basically no knowledge to produce and promote T-shirts online. But I did it all wrong. There was no logo, no consistency in the branding, no identity. I also printed way too many shirts with the worst size scale ever, and I had absolutely no infrastructure. My Instagram comments were full of complaints. I'll never forget, at one point I just refunded every customer because I couldn't fulfill the orders in time.

While the Cookies business wasn't off the ground yet, the Cookies strain had caught on big-time from all the great buzz, and many rappers were reaching out to get some for themselves. I was able to parlay that in a couple different ways. One was a last-ditch effort to save the clothing company. I had a show with a great lineup at the Bill Graham theater with Wiz Khalifa, Schoolboy Q, and a few other heavy hitters. I designed a T-shirt that I wore onstage. It was black with a big green crest across the chest that read "Golden Gate Harvest Club" with a bunch of marijuana leaves surrounding the text. I had a thousand of them made, figuring fans at the show would eat it up once they saw it. I ended up selling nine of them. Nine! I took the nine hundred and ninety-one shirts, left them in a friend's warehouse, and threw in the towel.

While the T-shirt biz seemed dead, my rap career, thanks in part to the connections I was making, seemed like another angle to get out of the game. I used the last of the money I had to make my third album at the Paramount recording studios in L.A.

Paramount had everything you could ever want. There were comfy leather couches, free snacks, and a runner—a dude who would get you anything you needed. I especially loved the SSL boards they used and the energy of the studio spaces; the dimmed studio lights set the mood just right. Most importantly, I knew it was a spot where popular people went. The way I looked at it, I could spend money going to the club and popping bottles, or I could go to this studio and actually run into the kinds of important people I wanted to meet.

I was in Studio B and, on this particular day, Chris Brown was in Studio A and CeeLo Green in Studio C. In the hallways, I ran into one of Brown's cousins, 'Tuan, who recognized me and invited me into their studio space.

I walked into the room and there was a faint smell of weed in the air and I heard one of CB's crew asking the runner to go pick him up a burger from Wendy's and fries from McDonald's. *What bougie-ass world did I just walk into?* But Chris and his crew were cool as fuck. Somebody asked if I had any Cookies, saying they all wanted to try it. Prepped for this moment, I took a few stackable mini-jars out of my backpack, all different strains. The second they laid their eyes on the weed, I knew I had them in the palm of my hand. I ended up smoking a few joints with them and left them with what few nugs were left, even though I had a half-pound of Girl Scout Cookies in my bag, and we exchanged numbers.

A few days later, 'Tuan reached out to see if I could get them some more. I got an idea. I asked him about getting Chris to do a feature on my album, and he agreed, saying they'd do it for $20K.

I knew I couldn't pass it up. I wanted to go huge, so I grabbed a beat and a hook from Big K.R.I.T. and got Wiz to do a verse. The song was "Yoko," and it single-handedly launched the Cookies brand.

I came up with a goal to shoot a music video and debut it at the top of WorldStar. I had truly given up trapping after Mom died, so I only had a little over $20K to my name, and it was buried in my mom's backyard, where I had planned to keep the rest of my cash before it was stolen. I would have nothing left, but this opportunity felt too good to pass up. My dad was over to visit, and as we stood in the kitchen I laid out the situation to him.

"Is the investment worth it? I can't afford for it to fail," I said.

"Follow your dreams," he told me.

So there I was, digging up my last $20K in the yard like in some mobster film.

Back at Paramount, when it came time for Chris to record, I was expecting a bridge or singing. Instead, he started rapping. I was worried, but when we hit playback on the big speakers the whole room went crazy. I mentioned the video to 'Tuan, who seemed dedicated to making it happen.

There was one catch—Chris's manager wasn't happy about my organic connection with Chris and was even less enthused about him featuring on my track. She didn't want to clear the rights, but like the name of this chapter says, "no" is just a means to negotiate. 'Tuan called me later that night and said that he would work on the manager and not to worry, that Chris loved the record.

"You know, Berner," he said. "If we can find a way for him to pull his Lambo out and go crazy somewhere, we might be able to convince him to show up and shoot his scene for your music video."

I was in "go" mode before he could even finish the sentence. If I could pull this off, it would mean the world for an underground artist like me. I can't explain why, but my first thought was, "What am I going to wear in this video?" I realized it would be an amazing opportunity to wear something that I owned. I took the blue Cookie logo that Shemp by now had designed and put it on a black hoodie that made it *pop*. This was the first use of it. My outfit was complete, but now I had a new problem: How in the fuck was I supposed to arrange a way for Chris Brown to drive his Lamborghini in this video? I didn't have the time or budget to deal with things like street permits—hell, I had no money at all. I had to get creative. I Googled "racetracks" and called up one in Orange County called Irwindale Speedway. An older man answered the phone, and I explained the situation and the $1,500 budget I had to work with. I've never heard the word "no" so fast. I asked him how long he would be at his office and if he minded me heading over to speak in person.

"Well," he said, "if you want to hear 'no' in person, then head on over." *Click.*

As I mentioned earlier, I don't drive. So I hopped in a taxi for the nearly two-hour drive from my apartment in Hollywood to Irvine. When I arrived, the man from the phone looked like he'd seen a ghost. He was around fifty years old, a semi-balding White guy, super square. He walked me past a handful of cubicles to his office, which had floor-to-ceiling windows that overlooked the grandstands.

"See that corner of the parking lot?" he asked, pointing away from the track. "Someone just rented that corner for an event and are paying thirty thousand dollars. It took months for us to work out the deal." Then he pointed to a huge Coca-Cola billboard and other major brand signs along the track. This was his way of letting me know I was living a pipe dream. Besides, it was almost 5 P.M. and he wanted to go home.

I asked him if he could just quickly pull up YouTube on his computer.

"This will take five seconds," I explained. "Search 'Chris Brown' and take note of the number of views."

He did. It was in the millions.

"OK, now search Wiz Khalifa."

He did, asking me what the point of all this was.

"Last thing," I said. "Search 'Berner.' "

He saw the number of views. "See the difference?" I asked him. I was speaking from the heart. "These guys are huge, hundreds of millions. I'm in the thousands. I'm just an underground artist. I need something cool that will motivate them to shoot this video with me. If I pull it off, this can change my life."

The man didn't say anything.

"Anyways," I said, "I just knew I wouldn't be able to sleep at night if I didn't at least come here and try my best."

I shook his hand, thanked him for his time, and turned to leave.

"Hey," he said as my foot stepped through the doorway, "be here tomorrow. You'll have one hour. And keep your $1,500. Just bring $500 for a medic. I'll see you in the morning."

Holy shit! I was in the game. I called 'Tuan and told him to let Chris know that he could do donuts in his Lambo at a professional racetrack. They were in. When we arrived the next morning, I couldn't believe what I saw. There were multiple race cars on the track and even an 18-wheeler cab he said we could use. The man at the racetrack said he'd called in a favor and had the stunt drivers who had driven in a Kanye West and Jay-Z video a few days earlier show up to perform for free. That alone increased the production value to a couple hundred G's at least. It turned out that the man from the racetrack had told his daughter about the shoot, and she was the biggest Chris Brown fan ever. All she wanted was a picture with him, and I suppose my guy just wanted to be the cool dad. He even had that eighteen-wheeler doin' donuts in the video. Beyond my wildest imagination.

The "Yoko" video wrapped, and it went *crazy* on WorldStar. Because I was already popping from all the weed content and now had this crazy music video featuring three massive stars in Wiz Khalifa, Chris Brown, and Big K.R.I.T., it instantly earned the top banner spot on the webpage, just like I had envisioned.

That day alone, 25 million people watched the "Yoko" video. They also saw the Cookies logo for the first time, and I knew then that I was finally on the path toward building something legitimate for myself and my family.

The other piece of the puzzle that I was trying to fit together in 2011 was how to move Cookies forward. One central thing was keeping me up at night: How could I trademark the word *Cookies*? The thing is when it comes to marijuana, you can't trademark anything federally. It's a concrete wall you can't run through. But you *can* trademark clothing, and you can trademark a logo. And when you're trying to get a brand off the ground, there are times when you have to get creative.

After doing some research, I learned that I could sell clothing that said "Cookies" on it and use a different name for the trademark. So, still bruised from my failed first attempt, I set up a website and put up ten hoodies for sale. On the tags, I put the Cookies logo and right below, in a much smaller font, added the letters "SF." As long as that "SF" was on that tag, technically I could sell my Cookies shirt under my own protected trademark, which is why my streetwear brand is technically called CookiesSF.

I prepared the hoodies, stuck the labels on strategically—they weren't even sewn on properly—and carefully took a picture. Then I let it it be known that the hoodies were available for sale on the website. With each sale of a hoodie I shipped, I included a proof of sale that featured the same CookiesSF logo that was on the clothing and the label. I hired a trademark expert who helped me complete an application to the trademark office, which included the photo I took and the proof that I was already selling the clothing.

Six months after I applied, the expert guy called me out of the blue to tell me we'd been approved for a trademark of Cookies. Boom! I was in the game and ready to rock.

. . .

A couple of months after my T-shirt fiasco and just after busting my ass to make the "Yoko" video with the first Cookies logo, I got a call from Matt. "Holy shit, you're not going to believe this," he yelled over the phone. "Get your ass over here *now*."

When I arrived at his house, he told me that he'd learned that Mom had left us an IRA, which came as a huge surprise seeing as how we thought she'd passed away with very little to her name. If I let the IRA mature, it would be worth $45,000 or so. If I were to cash the IRA early, I learned, it would be worth $19,000. You wanna talk risk?

I was so close to cashing the check, buying some packs, and flipping them to double, if not triple, my money. That would have been easy. But my gut told me to ignore that instinct. Instead, I ended up at Wells Fargo in downtown San Francisco. Walking through the heavy doors into the marbled bank, I looked around at the other customers and wondered if they'd ever had to bury their money underground. I should have felt like a complete outsider. But I didn't. I felt like I could belong in any room, and I still carry that belief in myself today. Be it the break room or the boardroom, I can fit in. I ended up opening the very first bank account for

CookiesSF, which would become my clothing brand, and put all $19,000 into it.

. . .

I needed to be smart about how to get this brand off the ground. I thought about exclusivity and what made luxury brands hot and decided to limit access and raised the price to $100 for the CookiesSF hoodie. I announced that I would only be dropping one hundred units at a time and hoped to hell that the terrible luck I'd had with everything else I touched in the clothing space was about to run out.

One minute. The hoodies sold out in one minute. This was the continued effect of the viral moment plus scarcity. In those sixty seconds, I made $10,000. The "Yoko" video put CookiesSF in front of the right eyes, and the initial sale proved that people craved the limited drops. I ended up repeating the same process with different colorways; each new print had custom drawstrings matching the logo, which felt like something new in streetwear. The new colorways sold just as quickly, and I knew if I was ever going to level up, the time was now. That's when I took the biggest risk so far: putting my business in other people's hands.

I set up a meeting with a guy named Chris Grunge, who owned a printing, design, and fulfillment company. With Chris, all my back-end issues were solved, and he provided better materials to print on while still allowing me to increase profitability. But working with a killer fulfillment company could only get me so far. So, as CookiesSF merch was selling out on the regular, I thought about taking another risk.

I heard about these guys in East Bay, Eric Fan and Charles Yang, who were a one-stop shop when it came to production. They were both a fair bit older than me—Charles was in his early sixties, a short man with close-cropped gray hair who spoke with a very heavy Chinese accent. Eric was about ten years younger than him but had a baby face and looked like he was still in high school. They were manufacturing hats, wallets, beanies, backpacks, and all kinds of other accessories for brands like ELEMNT, Chocolate, and Diamond Supply. I got their contact info from Al Freshko and reached out about wanting to make my brand look bigger than it was. I told them that they were capable of changing my business overnight. But they explained that they were being approached by prospective clients daily and weren't really interested in taking on any more. So you know me, I got creative. My pitch was this: Why continue to build other brands? Why not have skin in the game yourself and be a part of something before it truly takes off?

I told them about the buzz I had from the weed side of things, my Instagram and star-studded smokeouts, showing them some of the viral videos. I also showed them the "Yoko" video and the soaring view count. There was no better time to get into the CookiesSF business, I said, sharing some ideas for future clothing drops, along with stoner accessories that I knew would be massive sellers if we ever brought them to market, like innovative rolling trays, stackable storage containers, and smell-proof backpacks.

My offer was simple: $100,000 for 20 percent of the company. They were in. I couldn't believe it. I put the $100,000 into a personal account, while the CookiesSF account I'd opened at Wells Fargo had grown to a couple hundred thousand at that point for working capital.

With Eric and Charles on board, the dope thing was, I never had to think about samples. Most companies set aside plenty of money for samples or small trial production runs. They also usually need to fulfill minimum order requirements—say, three hundred pieces or more—and can get stuck with unsold inventory. Not us. With the manufacturers as my partners, I was able to produce a sample at cost, post a picture of it on social media, and gauge people's reactions in real time based on their comments. If people seemed to like the sample, we'd do a 75- or 150-piece run and sell it out fast.

Seemingly overnight, I went from the hyped hoodies to dope-ass bucket hats, belts, you name it. Then the smoke accessories hit the market, and it was game over. Products like the rolling tray with the slide-out ashtray and compartments for your lighter and paper, the stackable jars with dividers on each level, and food-grade seals to keep weed fresh had us jumping.

In the first year of my partnership with Eric and Charles, CookiesSF made two million dollars in revenue. We were doing great with online sales, and we had a small network of clothing boutiques carrying the brand. A ton of smoke shops wanted to carry our clothing, but I took a huge risk by turning them all down and keeping CookiesSF a high-end, exclusive streetwear brand. But deep down I knew there was still plenty of money being left on the table. There was a major piece of the pie missing: wholesale.

By the end of 2014, CookiesSF was buzzing. The brand had gained global popularity and we opened our first flagship store on Haight Street in San Francisco. Customers were camping outside for three nights before the grand opening. I would roll by at night with pizzas, hot chocolate, and, of course, herb. It was a total celebration, man. In the first few days alone we had thousands of people come through the doors.

One of them was a guy named Bryan Wilson, who was friends with one of my partners in the Haight Street store. Bryan was a well-known sales rep who'd worked with some of the most popular brands around, from LRG to Stance socks. His father had also been successful in the fashion industry in the '80s. When I learned what Bryan did to help take those companies to new heights, I knew exactly what I needed to do.

I set up a lunch meeting to convince him to come on board as our sales rep. He explained that he wasn't looking to leave his position, where he was on salary and making great commissions. But, like Eric and Charles before him, I knew Bryan didn't have skin in the game. So, knowing how a rep like Bryan could grow our business, I gave him the same pitch that I gave them. I explained how CookiesSF was growing, that we had just done a collab with LRG that went into the clothing store Zumiez and sold crazy good, and that we had just turned down a five-million-dollar acquisition offer from a competitor. He seemed impressed. I offered Bryan $75,000 and 15 percent in CookiesSF that would vest based on performance and goals. He was hesitant, but deep down he recognized our potential; the hype we were receiving was undeniably unique. We shook hands and never looked back. With Bryan in the mix, revenue for CookiesSF soared to five million the next year. Within two years we had reached eleven million dollars and in year five we hit the fifteen-million-dollar mark.

In 2021, CookiesSF generated fifty-eight million dollars in revenue.

I gambled on myself, engaged in nontraditional business deals, and took massive risks at each and every step. It's how I took a $19,000 investment and turned it into more than a hundred million dollars in revenue. CookiesSF is one of the biggest streetwear clothing lines out there; that it is still as relevant today as ever is absolutely epic.

In negotiation, sometimes the answer is a soft touch, and sometimes it's brute force. Take a recent example: I had a friend visit me in L.A. from out of town. I wanted to give him an experience and take him to Jon and Vinny's—a hype beast restaurant in the city.

The Kardashians eat there, paparazzi out in front, the whole nine. We pulled up for lunch, and I asked for a table for two. The hostess explained that they were booked solid all day. "You're welcome to wait here to see if something opens up," she said.

"Hmm. You see, I got my boy here," I replied, "and I'm really just trying to show him this spot."

"Sorry, we're all booked."

I walked outside and took $500 cash out of my wallet. I quickly folded it into a square and put it in the palm of my hand.

I went back into the restaurant and told her straight up, as I shook her hand, "Listen, I got five hundred dollars in my hand." I've worked in restaurants; I know how much money that is. I put the cash in her hand and asked again. "Please, can we get a table? I'd really appreciate it."

She thought about it.

"Do you know what you want?" she asked.

"I do—two orders of the six-hour beef bolognese, a wedge salad, and we'll take some meatballs on the side."

"I'll go put in your order now."

The chef brought the food out himself. They even gave us free drinks. And anytime I go there now, I don't have to worry about getting a table.

I've used this move a lot. In Vegas, at the Japanese restaurant Mizumi, I gave the hostess $300 on a crowded Saturday night and got a table. In Chicago at Au Cheval, the trendiest burger bar in the country, there was a three-hour wait. "Brother," I said to the host, who was this young dude in dreads, "I got two hundred bucks in my hand. Can we sit down?" I shook his hand and said, "Feel the money?" so he knew to take it.

At the end of the day, it comes back to understanding humans. You'll notice that, when it comes to overcoming "no," these aren't examples from the boardroom—and that's the whole point. In your personal life and in your life as an entrepreneur, you are going to encounter "no" . . . daily. What you do with those speed bumps is up to you. Do you give up when you hit a wall? Or do you find a way to get through to the other side?

Even something as basic as trying to land a table at a packed restaurant can be an opportunity to hone your skills and work on dealing with people and turning a "no" into a "yes." Every single day is an opportunity to practice and learn.

No risk
No reward
GELATO *

Chapter 6

NO RISK, NO REWARD

Being an entrepreneur is like a fucked-up roller-coaster ride. Imagine one like the Drop Zone that lifts you up only to send you on a free fall toward the ground. The anxiety as you climb, mixed with that strange calm before the big drop. The rush on the way down and the breath of relief when you're safely exiting your seat. That's basically how I describe a typical day on my phone.

Being CEO, creative lead, and the face behind a company requires so much time, energy, sacrifice, and, inevitably, an incredible amount of risk. The ride is addicting, and it's hard, maybe impossible, to turn off that part of my brain. Restless nights with monkey brain start to feel like powerful strategy sessions, and staring at the wall at 4:45 A.M. while the next great idea percolates has become normalized. I even find myself strategizing as I walk up and down the hallway in the middle of the night with my infant baby trying to soothe him and get him comfy and back to sleep. If you want to win, you gotta be all-in.

My boy Stinje always reminds me that I like to take the long odds. He's been a fly on the wall for the last twenty years and has reminded me, whether it be music, clothing, my rolling paper brand, building Cookies, or even now as I enter the film space, I've always been extremely hands-on and invested my own money into my passion projects—even when it was my last. It's been the case in pretty much every venture I've started.

Some might call it gambling. I see it as the best way to make something happen. If you invest your own money into something, I promise you will do everything in your power to make it work. It's a different kind of drive. In business, there are risks around every corner.

. . .

With the streetwear business getting off the ground and the Cookies strain absolutely popping off, it felt like the right moment to make moves again in the weed game, but this time on the legal side. The legalized cannabis industry, I would learn, is one of the most cutthroat businesses out there. Imagine the dotcom era but with more gray area. An industry that was built around a sense of urgency and uncertainty of the future. A litigious world where small amounts of capital can create major turbulence.

I thought I had put myself on the line and risked it all getting CookiesSF off the ground. It had been a hell of a ride. Turns out, that was just the beginning.

. . .

The first opportunity came back to the Hemp Center. It was around January 2014. I had just finished putting my lunch order in when a small, quiet man we knew as "Asian Jay" walked through the front door. Jay was a vendor at the Hemp Center and ran his own dispensary in San Jose. He'd show up to see what we were carrying or to sell us product or to show us batches of this wild tea mix he used to make. He would chop it up with the Hemp Center staff and show us some new product he was carrying in an overstuffed backpack. We smoked a couple joints and ate our lunch before Jay dipped out. On his way out the door, he pulled me aside.

"Hey, Berner," he said, "you want to make some extra money?"

I told him I was all ears.

"You know that 'Cookies' logo of yours? I'll give you $2,500 per month if you'll let me paint the logo on the wall of my San Jose store."

I hadn't even considered anything like that. But why not? I said sure, as long as Jay would begin carrying and selling the new Gelato and Sunset Sherbet strains. He agreed so fast that it almost made me suspicious. Either way, we had a deal.

Within a month, Jay was running the most poppin' spot in San Jose. There were lines around the block, and my hoodies were displayed for sale in the front lobby. Snoop Dogg stopped by and took pictures in front of my Cookies logo on the wall, and Wiz Khalifa even shot a music video in the store. That shit was jumping, so much so that it started to become a problem. Neighbors began complaining to the city about all the commotion happening at the Cookies store—that's right, they were calling it "the Cookies store."

It was pretty obvious that between the herb I was supplying via the crew, my merch selling off the shelf, and the Cookies branding, my $2,500 per month was hardly a fair deal anymore. But I saw the value in the hype, the proof of concept, and the free marketing it was getting. Shit, that authentic word-of-mouth hype had always driven the popularity of the "Cookies" strain.

Eventually, our genetics were leaking out to growers and showing up everywhere. Even Asian Jay paid one of Mario's employees for a cut of Gelato and Sunset Sherbet, and he had started mass-producing it without paying me or the homies anything. My team would get so mad at these kinds of leaks, and I get why, but I was kind of juiced, to be honest. The way I saw it, we were getting our name and genetics out to the whole world. People started to become fans of the Cookies Fam and were respecting us through our work and giving us props on social media. The hype machine cost us nothing, and we had zero risk. I looked at the leakers as our cheerleaders. They were doing all the work for us. And it helped make us industry leaders and trendsetters.

By the end of 2015, the name "Cookies" was everywhere. The weed was buzzing so hard that it made the merch pop. The merch buzzing helped make the weed pop. And the music was fueling both. It was all feeding into each other. As focused as I was on building my clothing brand and making music, something bigger was happening that was too magical to ignore.

. . .

We had the genetics. We had the hype. We had the megaphone. My experience at the Hemp Center and my many years in the game gave me the knowledge I needed to truly understand the customer in the cannabis space. Plus, I had a serious market advantage over others, thanks to my rap career and the Cookies clothing, for which I'd filed a trademark covering the name and the logo. I had all the ingredients to go legitimate. But I was a street guy. The idea of owning a medical marijuana dispensary scared me, and I knew if I was going to capitalize on a cannabis industry that was about to explode, I had to do it differently. Nothing about the next steps of growing the cannabis side of my Cookies empire was easy. I had to learn the hard way how dangerous putting your brand in someone else's hands truly is.

It wasn't long after Asian Jay's store in San Jose took off that I had people approaching me from all over looking to replicate the success; clearly, I was learning, there was tremendous value in proof of concept. There was a dispensary in Sacramento that wanted to carry Cookies and other strains the crew was developing and popularizing. I met with one of the owners, a man on a mission, who showed up in a really tight shirt and even tighter pants, long before either were fashionable. I later learned that the guy was a legend in the world of pick-up artists; his nickname was Minotaur. He was sharp and was always straight and to the point. I told him it would cost him $5,000 per month, and I would need to be paid in three-month installments. He agreed without hesitation and arrived at a coffee shop the next day with a heavy white bag with $15,000 in cash, all in twenty-dollar bills. As I took the bag from him, I knew this was just the beginning.

. . .

The medical cannabis industry in California was big business in those days before weed was legalized for recreational use. *Anybody* could get a medical card, and everybody had one. All you had to do was say you had a headache, pay twenty-five bucks, and boom, you had your card.

As the calendar turned to 2016 and the demand for our genetics grew, the opportunity to carve out a corner of this growing market was too good to pass up. Recreational cannabis had just been legalized in the states of Colorado and Washington; if Proposition 64 passed, California was going to be next. I knew we needed to do something quickly and plant our flag. And I had a plan.

We, the Cookies Fam, had been really focused on breeding. We had so many exotic genetics, and they were all unique in their own way. But we kept running into the same problem: How do we know which ones to keep and produce? One of the hardest things to do, even today, is to select the different strains and know you've made the right choice, which inevitably means throwing some promising strains away. (Even as I write this, there are seventy-five jars arranged on a conference table in front of me, and a lit joint is hanging from my lips as I take note of the taste and smell.)

Mario and I got to talking, and the idea of doing a private tasting event came up. Our friend owned this dive bar on the outskirts of San Francisco, which would make the perfect venue. First, we took the genetics to one of the first testing labs in the state and got each one tested. We figured out the percentage of THC (tetrahydrocannabinol, the psychoactive compound in weed that is responsible for the feeling of being high; usually—but not always—a higher percentage of THC means a stronger high), cannabinoids (which determine the chemical structure of the plant), and terpenes (which give the weed its distinct smell)—the DNA of the weed. This was all still pretty new technology at the time. We printed out all the results on handheld cards. Next, I strategically invited a who's who of dispensary owners, trappers, industry folks, rappers, and more.

On the night of the tasting, the event was such a vibe. It was dimly lit and smoky as fuck, big clouds of herb hovering just below the ceiling. We had the different strains and flavors laid out on tables in jars with magnifying glasses above each of them so you could see the detail of the bud and its trichomes. The jars were all labeled—*Gelato 3, Gelato 24, Gelato 33, Gelato 45*, all the different phenotypes, which are the different seeds we had popped using the same parents. Today you can walk into a million dispensaries that display their product like this, but at the time nobody had ever seen weed presented like this. It was innovation at its finest.

Each guest was given a blank card that read "Gelato Tasting," with all the different seed types listed, along with categories like "aroma," "taste," "high," and "bag appeal." The guests were asked to give their score from 1 to 4 for each category. We created this community-based tasting and selection of our menu. As far as I knew, this had never been done before. We were having fun nerding out on the weed, but it was epic, and the event brought us legitimacy. And—you know me—I documented all of it on video.

At the end of the night we collected the scores and used the results to narrow down our selection, creating our menu right there on the spot. If you're not already in the cannabis industry, you may not understand what happened that night, but believe me when I say this was history in the making. From the tasting, we ultimately selected Gelato 33, Gelato 41, Sunset Sherbet, and Gelato 45. Those strains would be our bread and butter, and to this day they are still the backbone of the majority of breeders' menus. Study the lineage of the strains from the biggest weed companies today, and you'll find their origins date back to the night of our Gelato tasting. We emerged from that evening with a staple menu, a brand-new concept of crowdsourced R&D. We felt like bosses. After the weed tasting, we brought out gelato ice cream for everyone before the entire party ended up at Nation's Giant Hamburgers in the wee hours of the morning. Stoned as fuck, burnt out, double cheeseburgers for everyone. It was amazing.

. . .

Among the guests I'd invited to the tasting was a man from Sacramento who had introduced himself to me a few months earlier and was looking to work with us now that he saw the hype Cookies was getting. He had a group (we'll simply call them The Group from here on out), and they were fired up about expanding their business using our genetics. Me and my crew were still growing in garages, but The Group was operating huge legal grows and chains of dispensaries. They knew we had something special if we could effectively produce our genetics at scale, and they wanted to become our official retail partner and brand their stores as "Cookies"—using my likeness in the process.

I began discussing a pair of deals with The Group.

The first would be a formal licensing deal with me, because I owned the logo and Cookies identity. I would use my social media presence to promote their stores, and The Group would have the freedom to use my likeness. This licensing deal, which was exclusive to their stores in Northern California, would see me getting paid $90,000 per month for the next five years. That's *five million dollars*. Fucking life-changing money for a guy like me—and I didn't have to build the stores or manage the cultivations.

The second was a deal with the crew to license our genetics to produce for their stores and establish a royalty structure that would see the crew earn $400 for each pound they produced. The Group makes, say, 600 pounds of our Gelato 41, we'd get $400 for each. Add that up and it's a lot of bread.

On Cloud Nine with my deal in the books, I approached the crew to talk through the royalty arrangement, which had the potential to earn us more than double—if not way more—what I was getting from my licensing deal. That was the beginning of the end.

The words were barely out of my mouth when the crew informed me that they had already finalized their own royalty deal with The Group that included a $75,000 cash advance to split among themselves—and nothing for me. "You're already making money off of your clothes," one of them said, "so it is what it is."

I was kind of tripped out. But, looking back, I shouldn't have been surprised.

The way we lived, like every other street guy, it was every man for himself. We were all thinking small at the time. We were just trappers. We all found our own ways to eat off of what we were creating. There was no structure or order. We were a bunch of people who sold, created, and loved weed. We were passionate about what we did and loved the breeding process but never thought that our work could get us to where we were at now. We didn't understand legitimate business and contracts, proprietary considerations, and all of that. We didn't know how to protect ourselves.

But also, I think the guys were insecure about how much juice I had. I didn't personally breed the strains, but I was the one who came up with the names; I was the one who branded it. I used my network and reach to blow it up, and I was the one selling it and getting it in the right hands. I set the price and kept it high and was the literal face of what we had created. I looked at myself as the leader and the one with the vision and the most business experience, but they didn't want me to negotiate on their behalf. And they ended up getting fucked in their deal. They were the best at what they did, but they weren't businesspeople. They were creators. Artists. They didn't know how to negotiate, how to leverage like I did. So they made their own deal with The Group. I think they were anxious about losing out on something and wanted to see it through on their own. Maybe they did it out of greed and wanting power. Or maybe they were trying to avoid giving me a cut, and it was as simple as that. In all honesty, I wouldn't have expected anything from them. I was happy with my deal, and we were brothers. I had just wanted the chance to negotiate the best deal for them. After all, nobody knew the true value of what we had like I did.

At first, the deal with The Group seemed like it was working out for us all. When they showed us the first batch of Cookies they grew, I couldn't believe how dialed in their facility was. The buds were solid and dark purple, consistently through the pack. The structure and smell were crazy, and it was the first time I realized the true potential of our gear, which The Group was producing using dedicated dry rooms and all the newest technology available. Even when they began using PGRs to grow—which is the equivalent of steroids for humans (and something we wanted to steer clear of because that shit is bad for you)—the streets were still eating that shit up.

But things started getting weird with The Group. The first sign of trouble was when they denied the latest batch of Sunset Sherbet that Jai and Mario had cultivated, saying they could no longer justify the cost based on the quality. The color wasn't all there, and the buds were lime green and never turned purple like they were supposed to, plus the nose was kind of off. Fact is, it was just a bad batch, which does happen; we're talking about a real plant, and naturally, not every grow is going to be the same. Pissed off, Jai and Mario brought the batch to a neighboring dispensary where they were happy to carry the popular strains, which totally violated the terms of the deal with The Group. Ego is a huge problem within the cannabis industry, and The Group was angry. They stopped paying royalties for the genetics, which they argued could never be legally enforced due to cannabis not being federally legal. The Group simply stopped paying. They also began making edibles and hash using our genetics, even though the deal was supposed to be for licensing flower only. The relationship between the crew and The Group was eroding fast, and bad blood was being spilled everywhere. However, because I owned the IP of the Cookies logo and they had my likeness, I remained stuck in my contract with them, which created major friction with the people I thought were my best friends.

The Cookies Fam was never the same after that. I was pitted

against them and took hits from certain people who didn't understand the situation and claimed that I stole Cookies from Jai and the rest of the crew, which was laughable.

Those are my brothers, and I'll never forget what we built together in those early days, what we each brought to the table. Today, we're cordial. I saw Mario recently and gave him a hug, and told him I'm here if he wants to work together, and that if he wanted help building his own brand, Sherbinskis, that I could help him out and had his back. That's just how I roll. The bad blood from our fallout came from people who didn't understand my motivations and my focus on making Cookies a household name. From people who didn't understand that I didn't want to do wrong by anybody. The rest of the crew went behind my back and did a deal without me. That was their problem. But the immediate fallout was tough. There was a ton of tension. I received hits from people online, and it took some time to recover.

In some ways, I folded under the pressure. Jai had been making some noise, saying I had stolen Cookies from him. I heard he was saying that shit behind my back, and I began feeling righteous about it. I phoned him up one day to try to make things whole. "You think I stole Cookies from you, bro?" I said. "That's what you're telling people? You want to tell the whole world that I did you wrong? One, I named it. Two, I created the logo and the brand. Three, I did all the work creating the clothing line that helped grow the hype. Four, I'm the person who found all these deals for us in the first place." There was silence on the other end. "But you know what?" I continued. "You want me to make it right? I'll make it right. Take it. It's yours. I'll keep the exclusive rights for California," I explained, "and the rest of the universe is yours, dog."

The way I saw it, I wasn't just protecting my name. I was protecting my morals.

I assigned him the Cookies trademark for the whole world, save for California. I took a huge risk and gave him the whole brand. He held the global trademark for years as legalization neared, as the rest of the Cookies Fam went their own way.

A few years later, as recreational cannabis was nearing legalization in California, I called Jai. We hadn't spoken in forever, and things were still tense. "Listen," I told him. "Weed is about to go legal here. Next, it's probably going to go legal around the world. What have you done with the Cookies brand outside California?" He told me he hadn't done anything yet. "Roll by my crib," I said.

When he arrived at my house, I had a contract in one hand and $75K cash in the other. "Assign the Cookies logo and trademark back to me. We'll be fifty-fifty partners, and I promise I'll take this shit to the next level." I knew what we were sitting on with this brand and what the combination of timing plus my abilities would do for Cookies on a worldwide stage. "To not be in your feelings, here's compensation." I showed him the cash. Jai told me he was going to think about it. In some situations, money talks. He returned the next day and took the deal.

Now it was just me and Jai. No Mario, no Flux, no Kenny. It was the start of a new era . . . almost.

. . .

The industry was growing rapidly in large part off the backs of our popular genetics. In 2016, Proposition 64 passed, and we were all waiting for the light to turn green on recreational cannabis in California. What was already a big business was set to explode. At the time, The Group was running four stores using the Cookies name. They were growing the Cookies genetics and had even claimed to have been Cookies in the body of some emails. I started to feel a certain kind of way about it, and when I learned they were fund-raising upward of $40 million using *my* name and brand, I knew I had to put my foot down.

But I was contractually stuck in my deal, which still had four years remaining on it. In an uncertain industry with an uncertain future—especially back then—I knew I couldn't just sit back and wait out my contract. *These guys think I'm not going to make moves of my own? I'm about to set a new standard for this industry. Just watch me.* I started talking to operators in Los Angeles—outside of The Group's jurisdiction—about opening our own fully branded Cookies stores in the rec market, with a brand-new menu. This would be the first official Cookies store where I would have a say in the creative control, the design, and the kind of menus we cultivated. (One of my big rules: No PGRs.) It was going to be nothing like The Group's stores, which were run like a flea market. High traffic, high volume, in shady neighborhoods. The stores were a mess and looked terrible inside. My stores, on the other hand, would be clean and beautiful, designed with taste and purpose. My plans were getting off the ground, and people were paying attention. When The Group got wind, they were upset. But so was I.

"I'm sick of you making hash and edibles, raising money using our brand, representing yourselves as executives in this company—all without permission," I'd tell The Group any chance I could. Deep down, I think they knew my stores would pose a serious threat to their business, and they began spreading rumors throughout the industry. "Berner is just a clothing guy," they'd tell whoever would listen. "He's not a weed guy." They started telling people that the Cookies name wouldn't be allowed once legalization came into effect because it was too kid-friendly. They made up plenty of other lies to discredit me.

They even ended up changing their stores' names and rebranded using the exact same colorway, font, and look as my Cookies logo—which briefly caused major market confusion. They were just waiting to get rid of me, and the feeling was mutual. The Group knew I wanted out and had bigger plans for myself and Cookies.

One afternoon, I got a phone call from the leader of The Group. "Listen, you're not happy in this partnership, and we're not happy in this partnership," he said, stating the obvious. "Our investors are super worried about the new Cookies store you're planning, so we can do two things: You can continue your contract with us and promote as usual. Or we can let you out," he continued. "But if we do, you can never use the names *Gelato 41, Gelato 33,* or *Biscotti* again," referencing a new strain I had selected and named that was gaining major traction. "Your payments will stop immediately, and you'll be free to do what you want."

I took the deal. The guaranteed money stopped. I could do nothing but watch as the two strains continued to explode in popularity. Losing those genetics after all the work and well-timed hype—right before California went rec—was a serious kick in the nuts. Imagine Burger King losing the Whopper.

But understanding the bigger play, I took the high road and walked away. As much as I enjoyed getting that black Mylar bag with $90K in dirty twenties every month, I wanted to put the destiny of my company back in my hands. And so I was free. Free to do my own thing with my own company. In retrospect it was the best decision I ever made—but at the time it felt like the diciest. I took a huge risk, giving them everything. But the way I saw it, I had gained serious momentum in the legalized cannabis space. I had been the megaphone and marketing machine that had put the Cookies name on the map in the first place, and I knew I could make it happen again. I had both feet in the door of a billion-dollar industry and all the motivation you could ever need to start my own company.

I think most people would have felt like they'd been played. But they had given me the gift of the money to fuel my real dream, and the way I looked at it, my eyes had been opened. I learned that **while monetary gains are killer and quick money feels great in the moment, there is a bigger picture.** The long play was to build a true brand. One that, if done right, could outlive all of us.

I gambled big-time by putting our genetics in someone else's hands, but I was able to gain global recognition from our work and show the whole industry what good genetics, proper infrastructure, and effective branding could do. I learned so much in that partnership and was able to wake up my game. I now saw the true value of what I was bringing to the table. In my industry, there is no blueprint. It's all trial and error. I gained a ton of knowledge, learned why it's crucial to find the right partners, and discovered the importance of never losing sight of the big picture and my vision, no matter how risky it seemed.

In 2015, before recreational cannabis was legalized in California and after the GSC strain and the clothing line had been poppin', I knew we had to get serious about taking the next step. It was a pivotal moment for Cookies. We were a recognized brand at this point, but with legalization coming at us, we were trying to formalize and start a real company. Jai and I met with Parker Berling, who had been introduced to us by a friend in common who thought we might be aligned. Parker had been part of building and selling a pair of tech companies to Oracle and Microsoft, which made him someone with real corporate acumen who could help us on the business side take our brand to the next level. But he was aligned with us on the cannabis side, too. As a hobby, he had purchased a farm in Humboldt County where he oversaw a small wholesale grow and had started a cannabis investment firm, Mesh Ventures, as a way to get deeper into the cannabis industry. From our first meeting, I recognized that Parker was super savvy, experienced, and one of the few people I knew who had a drive that could rival mine. *I need someone like this on my team.* He offered to invest $5 million through Mesh, $2.5 million to go to me and $2.5 million to go to Jai. But right before the deal closed, Jai got squirrelly and told me he wanted to go another route. He had found another guy who showed interest in investing in Cookies. He brought me through to meet the guy at a packaging facility and explained how this partner wasn't going to give us money but instead was going to give us all these assets that, over time, would equal X amount in revenue. Blah, blah, blah. I just *knew* it was all bullshit. "Man, I don't feel good about this," I told him. It wasn't adding up, and it wasn't what we needed to grow our business. But Jai was adamant, and I didn't have it in me to argue with him—this time.

I went back to Parker. "Listen," I told him, "I know our deal fell apart and you weren't able to invest in Cookies. But I really want to work with you, and I think we can do incredible things." I told him about another brand I was developing—Lemonnade, my signature sativa brand. I showed him the menu of unique genetics and the bold logo and explained the concept. I told him that I wanted to get it off the ground and thought he'd be the perfect investor. I'd had my heart set on the $2.5 million I lost out on in the original deal, so I said, "Instead of investing $5 million for a small percentage of Cookies, we can do a deal where, for $2.5 million, I give you 40 percent of Lemonnade and we rock together." And then I explained the long game. "We both know Jai picked the wrong deal, and once he realizes it, the Cookies deal will fall back into your hands." To Parker's credit, he took a huge risk and took the deal. His fund had five or six million bucks to invest, and he gave me $2.5 million for a brand that had never launched before.

Thanks to that investment, I was able to start a business with Parker and his group. And I was able to buy the home that I still live in today. Parker turned out to be a wildly effective partner. We worked well together, and Lemonnade started moving fast—faster out of the gate than Cookies ever did. Parker was applying what he called an asset-light, capital-efficient business model to Lemonnade, one that he made clear he thought we should pursue with Cookies. It kept our overhead costs low and focused on working with handpicked operators who had already developed a supply chain. It was brilliant. When Jai saw what was happening with Lemonnade and asked what was going on, I told him that he'd picked the wrong partner. Eventually, within a matter of months, the Cookies deal ended up falling back to Parker.

I was in the driver's seat as I embarked on opening my first recreational cannabis store in L.A. It was shaping up just as I'd envisioned: a beautiful, purposeful, consumer-oriented retail space with our grow located in the back of the store. The first Cookies cannabis store, armed with a micro-license that would allow for retail, cultivation, distribution, and manufacturing all under the same roof. In any space that is brand-new, you have to find your lane and own it. I had to learn this all the hard way, and believe me, I'm grateful that it's the only way I've learned my whole life. No risk, no reward.

I took the risk, and now my reward was having the motions in place to raise capital, surround myself with a solid team that respected and understood the vision, and build the Cookies brand.

8360
8360
Cookies

Chapter 7

DON'T LET BLUEPRINTS BLUR YOUR VISION. CREATE YOUR OWN.

There was absolutely no blueprint to build a brand or company in the cannabis industry. Cookies could have never been born out of traditional business models or from the minds of typical marketing teams or C-suite executives. So many of the companies that formed after Prop 64 passed in 2016, which opened the door for the sale of recreational cannabis, followed a conventional model—and failed.

The legacy industry didn't fare much better. They may have had knowledge of the plant, plus a respect for and understanding of the culture—which is crucial if you want to resonate with your customers—but the legacy industry wasn't used to marketing or branding, and ultimately, this limited their reach. Besides, owning and operating a business, maintaining employees, setting up a retail shop, and navigating regulations proved to be way too tough for a majority of cannabis start-ups. Believe me, I've seen a ton of seriously talented people walk away from it all. You can be an incred-

ible cultivator and grow some of the best weed in the game, but to go from selling to a few friends or a small network to being able to serve the entire world requires a fresh approach.

While some aspects of my company resemble a standard consumer packaged goods (CPG) business, I recognized early on that there are unique and cultural differences with cannabis. To make Cookies work took knowledge of both weed culture and business, along with nontraditional marketing tactics, an open mind, and a vision to stray far from the textbook approach for building an enterprise and create something that had never been seen before. With Cookies, I found my lane and let creativity and innovation drive the boat. I never let existing blueprints blur my vision, and neither should you.

. . .

In October 2016, my best friend, Stinje, and I hopped on a flight to Seattle to film an episode of my YouTube series, *Marijuana Mania*. It's a true insider's deep dive into the birth and rapid growth of the recreational cannabis industry, which was really beginning to skyrocket.

Four years earlier, in 2012, voters in Washington and Colorado chose to legalize recreational marijuana, making them the first states to do so. It was a massive moment and the biggest victory so far for the legalization movement. The day Washington legalized weed, I was performing at a concert in Oregon with Method Man and Redman. When they announced the news to the crowd, the place went *crazy*. I'll never forget the energy of everybody being super juiced about the progress being made. It was about time! The world was ready for it, and marijuana had been unfairly cast as a dangerous underground substance for far too long.

By the end of 2016, eight states were on board. That year, the state of Washington by itself produced 59,394 pounds of white label weed (which refers to marijuana grown legally under a state-granted license), and the legal weed market generated $769,112,791 in total sales. With my profile in the rap game growing, the Cookies streetwear line *poppin'*, and Cookies genetics generating lots of hype in both the white and black markets, I knew we were on the brink of something massive. Just a few weeks after our trip, California passed Prop 64 and joined the party. There was actually a surprising divide among legacy operators in the lead-up to Prop 64. Those who had been running dispensaries for over a decade feared that recreational weed companies would put profit above product and that widespread legalization would lead to an oversaturated market, which is exactly what is happening nowadays. The cannabis industry is also being stalled by the lack of federal legalization, which is the next step for marijuana in the United States. I think it can happen in five to ten years but will have to be brought about by the next generation of politicians after the old gray hairs are out of office. But back then this all seemed like a pipe dream.

In Seattle, we landed at a private airstrip outside the city. After checking out some top-tier facilities and meeting with local growers who were meticulously cultivating Cookies strains, we headed to Belltown, a hip area by the Pike Place Market with a ton of foot traffic, to a dispensary called Have a Heart. The owner had offered me the empty retail space next to his shop, for free, to open a Cookies clothing and glassware store, which helped to bring more customers into his dispensary next door. Because cannabis retailers in Seattle weren't allowed to use traditional advertising like billboards, he had to get inventive. When we pulled up to the dispensary, it was full of life, with people flowing in and out of the doors. Before we got out of the car, I took a hit off a joint and took in the scene. There, right alongside markets and mainstream retail places—clothing stores, cafés—was this jam-packed store selling weed over the counter. It wasn't just normalized; it felt like it *belonged*. It was cool as fuck to see. There wasn't a security guard with a gun under his seat out front. The customers all seemed so happy. The vibes were immaculate.

To be able to simply walk through those doors and buy marijuana felt amazing. Once inside, I was handed a menu so big it made the Cheesecake Factory's menu look like a leaflet. All the product—flower, pre-rolls, oils, edibles—was behind glass, so you couldn't touch or smell the weed. In a lot of cases, because of the packaging, you couldn't even see the bud, so you ended up depending heavily on the package design to make your order (I remember buying an eighth of some random indica just because there was a picture of Willie Nelson on the cover). There were budtenders roaming around to help out and offer recommendations. It was a great experience, and I left with some great boutique herb and a smile on my face. But I also identified a few things I would have done differently. I left town with a fresh and gratifying perspective on how weed could exist in mainstream society . . . and with a clear vision for *exactly* how I wanted my stores to feel and function. I set out to create a blueprint for the high-end cannabis experience.

Two weeks after our trip, Prop 64 passed in California. But it would still be another two years until Los Angeles permitted recreational dispensaries. That's where I was going to plant my retail flag first.

. . .

On January 16, 2018, the first real Cookies cannabis store opened in the city of Maywood in L.A. County. The line snaked around the neighborhood block, and multiple news stations showed up to cover the opening. The mayor of Maywood was even there to help me cut the ribbon. A few years later I found out that, on top of being a nice guy, he was up to some serious shit and was arrested as part of a corruption case. What a world.

This store was the first one I opened after walking away from the deal with The Group, giving up some of our earliest, most popular genetics in exchange for getting control over my brand back again.

And while we didn't have our staple genetics for the opening, we had our brand and a place to call home in this massive stand-alone building in Maywood, painted, of course, in Cookies blue. We also had multiple breeding projects in the works to create a new menu. The future was bright. I had regained the brand, and the Maywood store was the first time I had full influence over the Cookies retail experience.

I put a ton of time and effort into creating a customer journey for L.A., one that has been replicated a million times since: The customer is greeted as they're checked in by a dedicated budtender who verifies their age before walking them to a table with our flower. The budtender is super knowledgeable and approachable, and their sole purpose is to stick with a customer throughout the journey. They're given time and space to look at the flower, prerolls, and edibles at their own pace. If they have questions, the budtender is nearby to help them with all their needs, and once they're ready the budtender takes the order on an iPad. From there, the customer heads to the register, where their product is waiting for them, and they finish the transaction with one of our cashiers. It can be intimidating to walk into a lot of dispensaries, especially if you're not a seasoned smoker. And that should never be the vibe. I don't care how good the Soup Nazi's soup is, if you feel on edge walking into any retail or service experience, then something is wrong. I wanted to make sure customers didn't encounter any barriers entering a Cookies store and were met by conversational staff to help put them at ease and establish trust. Eighty stores and lounges in eight countries later, and it's still how all our retail spaces flow. Matter of fact, this became the blueprint and industry standard for the retail cannabis experience.

Ultimately, I drew on my time at the Hemp Center. I really wanted to re-create the great vibes from back in the day after Prop 215 passed, allowing for medical marijuana. The way our budtenders serve a customer is in some ways a re-creation of the attention and care patients would get at the Hemp Center. That customer-first approach also extends to the people we work with and the sourcing of our product. It's about finding good breeders and passionate people who are great at what they do. It's about working with growers who have cultivated weed for a living for many years and have a wealth of experience in the business and maybe even worked with medical stores back in the Prop 215 days. I developed those relationships, and when it was time to open my shop I wanted to put them in a good position where they knew their craft was valued.

At the Maywood opening, I took it all in. Those blue walls, the immaculate retail floor and professionalism that had been missing in the stores that were opened by The Group, which had the Cookies name slapped on the outside but felt sloppy and disorganized. I observed the budtenders guiding customers through their journey, the smiles and happy faces entering and leaving the store. It felt so good to see the brand represented right.

The opening wasn't only a success; it was an eye-opening moment for me. Empowering. On top of putting an end to any confusion with my brand and The Group—which had falsely claimed in the past that they were owners of the business—it was validation that I could negotiate deals for stores and cultivation myself and retain all the equity in the brand. The next move, I thought, would be to put Cookies to the test and create a proof of concept that would take my brand to another stratosphere.

One day soon after the opening, I received a phone call from one of my partners in the Maywood store, a short Armenian dude named Alex.

"My brah-ther," he said in his thick Armenian accent, "I have an incredible opportunity for you." He invited me to lunch and pitched me on a storefront on Melrose Avenue in Hollywood. He was going to be the owner and pay me a licensing fee, while still allowing me to take control when it came to designing the store and ensuring it met the new standard.

Alex had to be the most confident person I'd ever met. Any question you asked, he'd answer with something like, "Don't worry, my brah-ther. One meee-llion percent it will be done." He was slick, but a sweetheart. He started out washing cars and somehow became a weed kingpin in L.A. By the time I met him he was riding around in big fancy whips and chain-smoking these skinny little Capri cigarettes. "Brah-ther," he'd say, "I'm trying not to smoke the beeeg ones." The guy was like a *Grand Theft Auto* character come to life. I liked him right away.

We wrapped up our lunch and went to tour the building, which stood on the corner of Melrose and King and used to be a super trendy restaurant, the kind paparazzi would be stationed outside of. Across the street was the iconic pink Paul Smith building, and the thought of having our blue building across the way would be absolutely perfect. But it felt too good to be true. I didn't know much about L.A., as far as the different neighborhoods went, but this one was clearly extremely wealthy. Nothing but bougie stores up and down the block. All I knew about Melrose was from watching *Melrose Place* with my mom as a kid. But I knew enough to know that planting a Cookies flag at this location would be a statement. The area was so nice that it felt unrealistic to even get a license to sell cannabis there, in front of a backdrop of couture retail and luxurious, celebrity-filled mansions. Most dispensaries were opening up in industrial areas like Maywood, or in downtown L.A. and the seedy parts of Hollywood. This was different. This was a prime location, real high-end shit. It was a flex to be there, and from the moment we left the tour I knew we had to make it happen.

But it seemed impossible. There were skeptics claiming that we would never be able to get the city to approve us, that we'd never be able to get that location properly zoned or to establish a license there. Alex never had a doubt. We applied for the license, and the longer we waited the more I was sure it was too good to be true. I'd call Alex: "Bro, are we gonna get this license?" He'd always answer, "One meee-llion percent, my brah-ther. One meee-llion percent."

While we waited for the city to approve, I got to work designing the store, including the circular flower table that has become the centerpiece of every Cookies store ever since. Competing stores would have a flatscreen TV on the wall displaying menus. Or else they would try to mimic an Apple Store, with dull wood tables with flower in display jars that masked the smell and made it tough to know what you were really getting. We custom-designed jars that not only allowed the flower to sit so it could be viewed from every angle—with a magnifying lens on top, so you could truly examine the bud—but could also twist open in such a way that you could smell the bud while still complying with regulations. Those jars were strategically placed on the circular table, which also included detailed information about the contents of each and every jar. Attached to the bottom half of the flower table in place of legs were stunning glass windows that we could fill with other products. The fact that I designed the table and built it, with zero renderings, with the help of someone Alex knew, an older Armenian man who spoke little to no English, still blows my mind.

Today you'll find our signature flower tables at the heart of every Cookies store. Apart from being a killer way to display product, the tables enhanced and helped to solidify the communal Hemp Center vibe I was going for. As a customer, while you're looking at the flower and edibles and vapes on display, you are literally creating a circle with the other customers and the budtenders. In that setting, the conversation becomes natural, and the environment is inevitably friendly. In other dispensaries, it's a fast-food experience. I wanted fine dining, with way more attention given to the customer. The table helped us bring a critical element of interaction, care, and knowledge to the Cookies experience.

Just as Alex had promised, our Melrose license was eventually approved (let's just say that I'll leave the story of how he landed the license for Alex to tell one day). We set about painting the entire building Cookies blue, with our logo dead center, and added a blue neon light that wrapped around the entire structure. I even added lights in the ceiling, like you'd see inside a Rolls-Royce Wraith, which felt fitting given where we were and the clientele we were expecting to shop at our store. This place was next level.

We opened on October 27, 2018—my thirty-fifth birthday. In the lead-up to the opening, we released teaser videos hyping the new location that had everyone talking. The turnout for this opening was beyond my expectations. People slept in front of the building for three days leading up to it, and again lines wrapped around the whole neighborhood by the time we were ready to open the doors. Many of my friends, including Wiz Khalifa, Logic, and B-Real, pulled up to celebrate, too, which got the crowd into a frenzy. It turned out to be far beyond a successful store opening. It showed the world what a Cookies store should look and feel like and set a new standard for the industry that others are still striving to reach.

We birthed our iconic look, designed our customer journey, and created a true destination spot in Los Angeles. I'd hear about people arriving to the store straight from the airport, luggage in hand. It became so popular that at one point we needed to open up a sister store down the street. For years, the Melrose location was our biggest store in the nation, and renderings of our iconic blue building even showed up in video games like *GTA V*.

By 2020, at its peak the Melrose store alone was doing $9 million a month in revenue.

. . .

As an entrepreneur, effective branding can be the most important tool in your toolbox. In cannabis today, branding is *everything*, and Cookies opened the door for the entire industry. Cookies was the first real brand in cannabis, and we forever changed the game and pioneered the way weed is bought and sold worldwide. We were the first to put logos on our baggies, which made our product an even hotter commodity. We were the first to kick off a successful streetwear brand alongside our cannabis company, the clothing serving as mini-billboards all around the world. In the process, I became the first face behind a strain, or brand. Walk into a Cookies store, and you'll be greeted by a collage of Polaroid pictures of me and all the different celebrities who flocked to our brand, similar to how a popular restaurant hangs photos on the wall of famous patrons who've enjoyed a meal there in the past. That's no accident. Those pictures are in restaurants so customers feel that the spot is exclusive, sought out by influential people, and, most importantly, of a high standard. I knew it was critical that people made that connection between our company and the passion and history I have for this business. Before Cookies got off the ground, weed strains would have names like Super Silver Haze, Trainwreck, Skunk, or Romulan. Go back a few decades further and you had your old-school strains like Colombian Gold or Panama Red. But at no point had there ever been a face or logo behind any of it—until I showed up.

Nowadays, the weed game is built around packaging and branding. In other words, your identity. Through Cookies, I learned organically how to build a brand. And I've since applied the same steps while creating identities for my other companies, like Vibes rolling papers and Lemonnade.

In designing the branding for Lemonnade, I wanted something powerful and timeless. *Lemonade,* like *cookies,* is an accessible, friendly word known to people around the world. It's a flavor that you can taste just by hearing the name alone, which instantly makes you nostalgic and transports you to your youth. The logo, which Al Freshko designed, is the word in the shape of a lemon. Because of the way it's designed—the word *LEMON* is the top half and *NADE* is on the bottom—we rolled with Lemonnade with two *n*'s. The packaging is bright and fun and looks great on our shelves—all reasons why the brand has done really well for us from the jump. Of course, it doesn't hurt that inside that dope-ass packaging is some of the tastiest sativa that's ever been produced.

Don't get it twisted: No amount of good branding can overcome a terrible product. Hell, your product *is* your brand. It's why I consider the quality control department—not the marketing department—the most important part of our company. I approach QC by putting myself in the shoes of the consumer. If I'm buying an eighth, I don't want scraggly little buds or bottom-of-the-bag shake. Those are like the cheap cuts of steak, and I want my customers to get the bone-in rib eyes. It's like going to McDonald's and ordering fries, and they're all soggy and the size of your pinky. You'd be pissed off, like, *What the fuck is this?*

As a connoisseur of bud, I know what I want my customers to find when they open our packaging. The bud needs to have good texture, it has to be sticky, not dry, with good bag appeal (the bud looks whole and inviting when you open the bag and look inside). It needs to be clean—no mold or bud rot (like any other plant or fruit, bud can rot if not properly tended). It has to have a good smell as well as taste, and it has to burn white ash. And it has to be cured right. Curing is the drying process and one of the final stages in the grow, when the buds are hung and air-dried in temperature-controlled rooms. Curing is probably the biggest issue most cultivators have—the drying and the storing—which takes time and experience, and the right facilities, to perfect. A lot of people can grow great bud on the vine, but most fuck it all up in the cure. So we look for very specific things when selecting the bud that makes it into our bag, like whether or not the plant stems snap once the bud looks ready—a sign of if it's ready to harvest. All these things I learned over time. It's like my whole life, from Daly City to Arizona to my time with the crew and the Hemp Center, was a real education in cannabis QC.

So we developed a standard at Cookies and Lemonnade where each eighth baggie needs at least three to five buds per bag. That ensures there is no shake or baby buds. The bottom line is: We respect our customers, and we want to give people what they are paying for. It's hard to oversee QC across a company our size, and you can't have eyes on every market. But we work closely with each cultivation partner to ensure that the same guidelines are followed across the board when cultivating and packaging our product. My QC team flies to different markets around the world and smokes new batches as they are harvested. At some point in the process, the samples find their way into my hands to inspect; in some partnerships, we turn down more product than we accept. Limited license markets can be tough; we want the brand present and hope to dial in any hiccups, but in some cases we have had to terminate entire contracts and lose market share due to quality issues. One day this will no longer be an issue for us, and we will have our own facilities. Hyper growth for any company is never easy; it's just part of rapid expansion and understanding the big play. The same is true for our clothing, where we examine every sample closely, everything from quality of material to how well the zippers work.

That quality control also needed to be there when we created Vibes, our rolling paper company, where we entered the space as a David among Goliaths—until we partnered with BIC lighters—in a heavily monopolized and gatekept industry. We needed strong branding that would set us apart from the rest of the shelf. You have big brands like Zig-Zag and Raw dominating the paper game, but to me they always felt bland. In many smoke shops they have a wall full of Raw brand papers, including all sorts of new products and sizes. Problem is, the whole wall is the same brown and red, all the packaging blending into each other, and you can't tell what is what. There could be as many as twenty different SKUs, but a customer wouldn't know it.

I thought about that missed opportunity when designing the look and feel of Vibes. The name is self-explanatory—everybody knows what Vibes is. You associate the word with talk of good vibes, good energy, something positive. I wanted a name that made you feel that. For the packaging, I drew inspiration from my childhood. One day back in Daly City during the Chinese New Year, a friend gave me an envelope with a couple bucks in it as a gift. I never forgot that envelope: It was ornate, painted red with shiny gold foil wrapped around it. When designing the brand, I kept coming back to that gold-foiled envelope. I had the idea of having a product line with multiple colors—red, black, green—all stamped with that gold foil. *That's* how you'd know it was a Vibes product.

I know how to organically build an authentic brand, and I have a sixth sense when it comes to marketing. I knew how to make noise around the world with Cookies, but I had absolutely no education on fundraising or growing a company. Sure, I picked up a lot of game while building my music business and clothing company, but the complexity of the regulated cannabis industry made me nervous. I'm an old-school street guy at heart, and I'd be lying if I said this whole new world of legal cannabis didn't make me paranoid. After all, I had a strong grasp on the market as it existed before, and the future, though bright, was still up in the air.

But with the momentum from the Melrose and Maywood stores, I was ready to keep the train going. I wanted to leverage the genetics, hype, and respect Cookies was creating while avoiding some of the major mistakes I'd seen other cannabis companies make. For example, there was a huge cannabis company called MedMen. They arrived on the scene just in time for Prop 64 and immediately raised hundreds of millions, if not billions, of dollars. They built massive grow facilities and hired tomato farmers to grow bud, which turned out to be of low quality and grown in such big batches that it would eventually become moldy. They were spending crazy money from the jump—I heard they spent $4 million for a single commercial—and made poor decisions every step of the way. They brought in big investors who knew nothing about cannabis and didn't care about quality or the customer experience. Just as quickly as they got off the ground the company crashed and burned. These fools were even parodied in an episode of *South Park*.

I saw where multistate operators (MSOs) like MedMen were going wrong—how they spent on marketing, built out oversized facilities with zero knowledge, and opened stores with no cultural influence or employees who genuinely cared about cannabis. And I had learned hard lessons from the deal with The Group and licensing genetics without getting paper'd up the right way. I took it all in and made a plan that informed how I would structure my business.

I didn't want to get diluted so early in my journey and lose control of Cookies. I needed to **figure out how to touch the world without raising hundreds of millions of dollars.** By 2019, Parker Berling had joined Cookies as president and held a seat on the board. Parker was a creative thinker who embraced going outside the box and executed some big ideas during the launch of Lemonnade. As we watched the success of the Melrose launch and began receiving a ton of interest in other markets, we started to discuss the different ways we could grow the brand. Originally, the two stores that opened in 2018—Maywood and Melrose—represented an equity play, and we held 20 percent ownership in each store. But we started rethinking our strategy.

We knew that we didn't want to be a retail chain. We simply didn't have the knowledge of how to secure licenses and, again, we didn't want to be in a position where we needed to raise a ton of capital. Instead, our thoughts were that we should focus on the wholesale. What if we could empower and leverage the hype of the brand and its genetics by partnering with both existing cultivators and store operators around the nation? This would keep us from having to raise a bunch of capital and could be our avenue to expanding relatively quickly. There was enough hype in the brand following the success of the Melrose location that it seemed everyone wanted to open a Cookies store.

Parker and I ultimately decided to change the deal for Melrose from a 20 percent ownership stake to a 5 percent license fee with a purchase option on the business, meaning we could roll up the assets with stock or cash at fair market value. This, we figured, would not only keep the operators extremely motivated but also kept our businesses non-plant-touching, which was crucial for our long-term vision (more on that in a moment).

I won't lie, it was hard for me to wrap my head around this at first. As a street guy, I'm thinking, "OK, I own 20 percent of this store that's raking in money, and now you want me to *not* own the store? And take 5 percent gross instead?" It didn't add up.

But Parker knew better. Once I understood the bigger play, I realized how genius this approach really was. Because all the costs are associated with revenues, the gross is actually a far smoother way to get paid. With a 20 percent equity position, owners and operators can claim all sorts of write-offs and expenses. Operators get creative in their accounting, and it becomes way too hard to collect money. With a 5 percent gross, everything is simplified. "You did $10 million this month? Cool, we get 5 percent." There are no questions asked.

Plus, when signing on with store operators, it's a lot easier to tell a partner, "We get 5 percent gross and you get 95 percent." It sounds way better than 80/20. But in truth it's actually better for us to take the 5 percent gross instead of the 20 percent equity position, because at that rate you almost never see a profit after expenses.

But that wasn't all. While we only took a 5 percent license fee on the stores, along with having a purchase option on the business, we also licensed our genetics—the world-famous weed we were creating ourselves—for a 10 percent license fee and we sold all the packaging to the cultivators who grew Cookies strains.

The result was the asset-light business model. We didn't have to worry about raising enough money to open a retail chain. We didn't have to sink a ton of capital into our growth. Based on the strength of our brand and the proven success we had out the gate, we were able to rapidly expand and soak in the rewards without any of the traditional risks.

With our asset-light model, we were able **to scale faster than most companies at a fraction of the cost.** While most of the top cannabis MSOs had raised anywhere from $500 million to $2 billion to expand nationally, we only had to raise close to $65 million, and we were able to put nearly all that money toward staff, marketing, materials, and other tools to help us grow.

The plan was working. By the end of 2019, operators had opened seven new stores using this model and were driving roughly $44 million in sales. We were growing extremely fast; every time we opened another store, we had more and more operators inquiring about the opportunity to open a Cookies store of their own. The beautiful thing about this is that it meant we were able to cherry-pick the best store operators who we knew would run their locations to our high standards. Cookies stores, under this model, are fully branded but don't exclusively sell Cookies products. You can liken it to a place like Whole Foods, which carries all sorts of brands. Our focus is simply on providing customers with the best products available; only about 30 percent of the inventory in a typical Cookies store are actual Cookies products. The way I look at it, weed drives the experience, not specific products, so we approach building our menus as tastemakers more than anything.

Same with cultivators. I understood how hard it was to build a massive grow operation. Cannabis is a living plant, and *so much* can go wrong in the process of going from seed to the final packaging. How do we avoid that? By finding quality people who are already cultivating and may be seeking our genetics and could use the boost in business that would come from working with us.

I love working with our farmers. We set up deals with seasoned cannabis cultivators who allow us to purchase based on batch, which helps ensure our quality control process remains a priority. Let's say I have a partner in Ohio cultivating for us. They pay for the facility, they pay for the grow, and the QC process removes any risk for us. If it doesn't pass QC, it doesn't go into Cookies packaging. Simple as that. That protection is built into the language of all our deals. Meanwhile, for most any other MSO out there raising all this money, if your weed sucks, then you're stuck with it, and you'll just have to find a way to sell it or eat massive losses. Not us.

I can't stress enough that not just anyone can cultivate for Cookies, and not just any operator can open a Cookies store. It isn't like a franchise opportunity that anyone can buy into. We're only interested in talented people who share our vision and passion for this business and industry.

Our business model has proven to be a win-win for everyone. Operators get a major boost in business when they paint their buildings blue and convert to a Cookies store. Plus, they get a chance to keep the majority of the money that's generated, while we gain a valuable presence in the market. Cultivators get a chance to grow and sell incredible genetics. (Sometimes we have to get creative in limited license markets like Louisiana, where there are only two cultivators in the entire state. In that case, we helped develop menus for one of the cultivators in exchange for "canopy"—space—in their facility.)

Changing our model from an equity play to a gross licensing deal propelled us further than I could have imagined. Because we were essentially an IP business and not a retail operator, not only did we eliminate a ton of the risk—and money—associated with retail chains, but it also left us with a non-plant-touching business, which was a major element in our strategy. Plant-touching businesses aren't permitted on the NASDAQ. With our asset-light model, we now had the ability to go public on the NASDAQ if we ever wanted to IPO. And while we only took in small royalties, at the time of a possible IPO we would be able to roll up all the assets into our portfolio—and the revenue associated with those businesses.

By 2025, Cookies had generated over $1.5 billion in sales.

The asset-light strategy was wholly unique in our space, and the results spoke for themselves. By 2022, we had opened 58 stores and were driving close to $300 million in sales. By the end of 2024, we had 77 stores with 188 partners operating in 37 markets. I firmly believe that Cookies is the most globally recognized cannabis brand in the world, operating in countries like Thailand, Canada, Israel, Germany, Portugal, England, Spain, and the Netherlands.

. . .

As a visionary, you can't expect anyone else to see what you see, especially in a brand-new industry. You have to create your own path, find your lane, and own it. When Cookies started to get off the ground, many people suggested I go the traditional route and hire executives from Coca-Cola or Nike to run the business. But what would they have brought to the table? What did they know about cannabis that I didn't? I followed my gut, embraced what I'd learned and experienced from legacy cannabis culture, and planted my flag in the ground like nobody had seen in the cannabis space.

Blueprints can blur your vision. It's why I was intent on writing my own.

Nontraditional marketing skills and inventive business models helped make Cookies the powerhouse it is today, and none of it would have been possible if we had not been looking for new models. While many companies spend crazy amounts of time and money trying to figure out market trends and what kind of products the cannabis consumer of the future may want, we tripled down on what people are actually consuming *now.*

Today you'll see plenty of cannabis brands trying to replicate what we've done with Cookies. Brands with clothing and accessories or packaging that looks and feels like ours. I go to weed conventions, and every other table is a new cannabis company wearing hoodies and gear featuring their logo. I see brands adding rappers as ambassadors to try to connect with key demographics. What I say to both young entrepreneurs out there and legacy industry folks is this: Find out what makes *you* special and unique, something that makes you stand out from the rest. This industry is still brand-new, and there's so much room for innovation. Also, don't copy. You're your own emerging industry and your own new model. **Always follow your gut, and don't ever downplay what you bring to the table.**

Chapter 8

NEVER BE AFRAID TO THROW BACK THE BIG FISH

By the mid-2010s, the media was referring to the birth and rapid rise of the regulated cannabis industry as the "Green Rush" and were comparing the growth of the legal weed market to the rise of broadband internet in the 1990s. Every major investor wanted a piece of the action. With the success we were experiencing amid the hyper growth of Cookies came plenty of potential investment and acquisition opportunities. From large multistate operators to international licensed producers—known as LPs—or even celebrity start-ups, you have to be extremely careful about who you take money from and when you should accept outside investments into your company. Timing is key, and not all money is good money.

Always perform due diligence on the people, companies, or investment funds that show an interest in you and your business. But it's still crucially important to listen to your gut. Try your best to read a person and their intentions before getting into bed with them. Big money can be alluring, but it's also scary, and people may try and use their fame or power to push through a deal that may not be favorable for you. Never let anybody take advantage of you because you're starstruck or attracted to their wealth and success. There are plenty of sharks out there who will try to woo you with one or the other. It's a tactic I've seen used many times in my years of doing business, be it in the entertainment or cannabis industries. So do your homework. Know your value. Never be afraid to throw back even the biggest fish.

. . .

As Cookies grew, there was no shortage of people who wanted to get into business with us. Parker and I took calls from tons of investors who wanted a piece of what we'd built, but one stood out above the others: a company I will call Sophisticated Investor or "SI." SI represented that they wanted to be one of the biggest investors in the space. Parker knew of the group behind the fund and the billionaire at the helm, who had also started a multibillion-dollar venture capital firm in Silicon Valley. They were one of the closest things to institutional capital investing in private U.S. cannabis companies. These guys were hella legit and brought instant credibility to our company. After connecting with the billionaire, I got the impression that he wanted to back us for all the right reasons. He told me he was going to take me under his wing and was going to mentor me, and that he could put me on a path to become a billionaire myself. *Go on . . .*

In the very beginning, when we brought SI in, they were friendly and believed in the brand. Their pitch was that they'd be my single-source capital partner and in 2019 made an investment of $10 million. I was being buttered up and told shit like "You're a baller, Berner. You're gonna be richer than Jay-Z!"

I thought their intentions were pure. I couldn't have been more wrong. The billionaire who headed this investment fund finessed me. He portrayed himself as a humble guy who wanted to see someone like me who came from honest beginnings win. He acted like he wanted to be my mentor, and even sent me a ballin' Traeger grill after our meeting. Plus, he invited me and my family to spend a week at one of his many lavish vacation properties so I could "clear my head." I remember it vividly. We pulled up to this humongous $20+ million property in Nevada right on Lake Tahoe that back in the day was a hangout for Frank Sinatra and the Rat Pack. It was the biggest, most elegant place you can imagine. It had everything you could ever want. Gym, theater, entertainment space, you name it. Downstairs was a fully loaded spa with multiple Jacuzzis and a fucking Himalayan salt cave with walls carved like Roman tile but made entirely of pink Himalayan salt. I spent a lot of time that week chilling in the salt cave, blasting old-school R&B and relaxing as best I could. In that cave, I couldn't help but start thinking, *If I get in business with these guys, maybe I'll be in this position one day.* I'm sure I wasn't the first entrepreneur who sat in that cave thinking those thoughts. I should have known the partnership was too good to be true. Turns out it was littered with hidden agendas.

While I know from personal experience that you can't dodge all bad partnerships, I'm grateful to have steered clear of a lot of the sharks who crossed my path over the years. When you're a pioneer and the biggest brand in an industry, you'll face this type of threat all the time. The saying "Mo money, mo problems" becomes more and more real each day, and litigation will begin to feel like a regular part of doing business.

. . .

The first time I turned down a sizable amount of money was an eye-opening experience, to say the least. It was 2013, three years before the sale of recreational cannabis would be passed in California, and our genetics were already dominating markets in states like Colorado and Washington, where it had previously passed. Cookies weed was buzzing in the streets and in medical markets. But as far as the brand went, this was still very early days. I was in Amsterdam with the original Cookies Fam—Jai, Flux, and Kenny Powerz—to be a judge at the 2013 *High Times* Cannabis Cup, which is like the Super Bowl of bud, where breeders from around the world bring their finest herb to compete against other cultivators. I had been traveling to the Cannabis Cup since I was nineteen and working at the Hemp Center. Back in 2008, I remember bringing what became staple strains like Granddaddy Purple, Sour Diesel, and OG Kush to Amsterdam, which helped me first gain a name for myself in the coffee shop community, where recreational cannabis existed pre-dispensaries. Now, we had flown out to the Netherlands to showcase our new menu and share our flavors with the local coffee shop owners. To get the product to the Netherlands, I had a Hemp Center employee ship a package to the hotel we were staying at. This sort of thing was always a risk, and it reminded me of when I was a nervous kid with an ounce taped to my leg boarding the plane from California to Arizona, but our system went off without a hitch. On that trip we introduced Sunset Sherbet, Girl Scout Cookies, and a few others, bringing our revolutionary California weed to a place globally recognized at that time as the mecca of weed. To have our own menu in my hands was a full-circle moment for sure.

This guy from Qatar named Mohamed, a friend of a friend who (according to rumors) had ties to a Saudi prince, had flown me out to Amsterdam a week before the Cup to hang and smoke. I was given $25,000, a stunning hotel room overlooking the canals, and a first-class flight there and back. Alongside Mohamed, we toured these beautifully low-lit coffee shops and stunted our new flavors, rolling joint after joint and causing crowds to form at each place we visited. The vibes were so good that, one night, I told my cameraman to start rolling, and we ended up shooting the music video for my song "Bad for Your Health" in a coffee shop called Joker and aboard a swaggy boat ride through the canals as we filmed around the city. The whole time, I could see Mohamed's wheels spinning. He knew that our goal at the time was to find a partner to open a Cookies coffee shop in Amsterdam.

We were in our bag and our name after just a few days there, and our brand was buzzing hard throughout the town. The day after we shot the "Bad for Your Health" video, I learned that Mohamed was actually about to become the owner of the Joker coffee shop we had filmed in. That evening, he asked for a sit-down with me and the boys. Over dinner, he proposed something that none of us were expecting. He laid out his pitch to turn Joker into a Cookies coffee shop and storefront. That was just the beginning. He also wanted to acquire the entire brand and offered us five million dollars right there on the spot. He mentioned additional opportunities for us to still earn royalties and whatnot off of seed sales and even proposed a separate investment into my clothing line, CookiesSF.

The excitement was real as we mulled over the deal later that night. So was the anxiety. As the rain began to fall from the dark sky, I could tell the vibe was starting to change. We ended up going back to the lobby of the Anantara Krasnapolsky Hotel, a dope spot with nearly two centuries of history. There we sat in the lobby, surrounded by ornate gold pillars and a grand stone fireplace, arguing for hours. I was so ready to make this deal happen. I had never imagined the possibility of having a million dollars to my name, and I didn't see the bigger vision just yet. Jai didn't want to go for it, and we didn't hold back on each other while we debated the pros and cons of selling it all. To me, at the time, it felt like a no-brainer. We'd have the backing of this wealthy dude, with even wealthier ties back in Qatar. We'd get a five-million-dollar check, with the opportunity to earn overseas and open a Cookies shop in Amsterdam. I didn't think it could get any better. Jai refused; he didn't want to commit. "I don't know, man!" he yelled repeatedly. His fear was that Mohamed was thinking too small, that the brand would only live in Amsterdam, where Mohamed liked to travel, and that would be the end of that. But to turn down five million dollars at that time in my life just didn't seem like an option. At one point, the hotel asked us to take it outside because we were disturbing the guests, so our conversation continued in the rain. Ultimately we reached the difficult decision to tell Mohamed that the deal was a no-go. I walked around the city at 3 A.M. staring down at the cobblestone streets, cold and wet as the weather reflected my mood.

When I spoke to Mohamed later that day to break the news, I could tell he wasn't used to hearing "no" very often. He was incredibly persistent; he shifted gears and focused on my clothing line, presumably as a way to eventually get his foot in the door into the cannabis business. Mohamed pitched the idea of opening a clothing store in both Qatar and Amsterdam and even wired $150,000 to my bank account to produce clothing for another store he was opening in Qatar. That's when it clicked: Jai was right. Mohamed *was* thinking small. At that point I had already been in discussions with Eric and Charles back in San Francisco to partner with me on CookiesSF. They were manufacturing practically all the poppin' streetwear brands back home, and I knew the value the two of them brought to the business as my partners. All Mohamed brought was capital. He didn't care about anything but owning the brand so he could say he owned it, to add a new toy to his portfolio. Here was a guy willing to write probably a one- or two-million-dollar check for CookiesSF. But since I was still relatively green in the clothing industry, I figured, *What's that capital going to do for me if I don't know how to make it work to build the business?* I needed strategic partners more than the money. The $100,000 Eric and Charles were giving me for 20 percent of the clothing line, while a fraction of what I could have gotten from someone like Mohamed, was worth so much more because of their established connections and experience in manufacturing. The hard truth was that Mohamed simply wasn't the right fit at that stage. After returning home I respectfully told him I wasn't interested in either acquisition he was proposing. I didn't hear from him again after that. He never even sent an address for the $150,000 worth of clothing he'd ordered.

By 2025, CookiesSF generated $100 million in sales to date. I'd say we made the right call.

. . .

It's one thing to turn down someone tied to royalty; it's another thing to turn down some of the biggest operators in the industry.

It was the winter of 2016 when I got off the plane in Edmonton, Alberta, and boarded a shuttle van for a three-hour ride to the middle of nowhere. As you can imagine, when California was going recreational, everyone was knocking on our door. At the time a handful of large Canadian LPs were making their way around Cali trying to find brands and companies to acquire in the space ahead of Canada legalizing cannabis nationwide, which ended up happening just a couple of years later.

I was in Alberta in the dead of winter to tour the facility of what at the time was the country's largest marijuana producer. It was fucking freezing cold like I didn't know was possible. My lips were dry and cracked for like a month after that. This Canadian company had an enormous cultivation site, by far the biggest in Canada and to this day probably the largest I've ever seen. And they were eager to acquire us.

As I toured the grow, none of it was making sense to me. There was a bunch of agricultural technology that wasn't well suited for cannabis, and the people in charge seemed to know nothing about cannabis. They didn't have proper dry rooms, and I remember in the middle of the grow room was a concrete drying safe big enough to hold three hundred people. From what I could tell, it was just way too hard to manage a facility of that size while maintaining any sort of quality. The whole operation was over the top. There was no way to oversee that much product from a cultivation standpoint—the curing process specifically was one of my biggest concerns. I knew almost immediately that they didn't know what they were doing and that they probably produced terrible weed. My read was that they had probably raised a bunch of capital and built up some plans that seemed impressive to someone with no background in the space and no real plan of how to use it. There was no functionality, and despite their massive size, as someone who knows what goes into making amazing, high-quality weed, it was hard to take them seriously. That's not to say that, when they offered me $800 million divided up into cash and majority stock to buy the entire Cookies operation, I didn't give it serious thought. But I didn't consider it for long. The facility tour had left a bad taste in my mouth. Same as when I met with the leaders of the company, and they barely even brought up the product when talking about growing the business.

I felt "pump and dump" vibes right away. They were talking

stocks, and I just sat there thinking, *When are you going to say something about the weed? Why aren't you talking to me about the genetics or explaining the next steps in dialing the facility in and bringing in great extract artists? What about growing the brand? Marketing dollars? Rollout plans?* To this group, it all seemed an afterthought. Cookies had to be built the right way, with passion for our flower at the heart of everything. Being under another company that from what I could tell knew nothing about cannabis wasn't going to work. With no plan on how to grow the brand beyond Canada and with no quality production that I could see, I felt the stock would eventually be worth nothing. I turned down the offer.

I might be delusional, I thought at the time, but I knew we needed to be in charge of our own destiny. What we had created in a relatively short amount of time, with no real infrastructure, was already making waves around the world. We had the potential to be the biggest brand in the industry one day, and this Canadian deal wasn't going to be how we got there.

By the way, by 2020 that company had announced losses of more than $3 billion. I knew what was up. I felt it in my gut and protected my business from a lucrative catastrophe.

. . .

Being pitched acquisition offers by wealthy jet-setters backed by royals or receiving offers close to a billion dollars from international LPs are rare opportunities. Far more common in an industry like mine are celebrity-backed partnerships and acquisitions. They can be tricky to navigate. I've had my fair share of conversations with celebrity heavyweights and almost drank the Kool-Aid a time or two.

The first major artist I had to turn down was Diddy. And, boy, was he persistent. Diddy had been extremely interested in Cookies and for nearly two years tried to set up a meeting with me. This was prior to all the allegations against him, but there was still something about him that made me uncomfortable, which is why I avoided him for so long. For over a year I would get voice and text messages from him; the dude also had bottles of liquor and other gifts sent to me on the regular. On July 19, 2021, I was chilling at my lake house in Montana, hanging by the water, when I got another voice message. He was clearly upset and told me how disrespected I'd made him feel. He'd had a market analyst reach out to me a few times through multiple channels, an extremely smart young guy who was studying the space, and I figured at least Diddy was trying to go about things the right way. He was obviously extremely influential in both the hip-hop and television space and had blown Cîroc all the way up. He had also moved mountains in the apparel world and had just been officially crowned a billionaire. All he wanted was a sit-down with me, and I relented. Burning bridges, especially with someone that powerful, is never good in business. I called Diddy from the dock in Montana to set up a meeting at his place in Malibu for the next day. I joked about him sending his plane to come get me. Without a hint of humor in his voice, he told me unfortunately it was being painted.

The next day I flew to Malibu along with the ultimate fly on the wall, Stinje. The rumors were already going around back then about Diddy being a superfreak. Something in my gut told me not to drink anything while we were there, so on the way to the Malibu estate, Stinje and I pulled over at a gas station and grabbed two big-ass bottles of water and pinky-swore with each other not to accept any drinks from anyone. I also made sure to schedule the meeting during the day and told him I had a hard out at 4 P.M. to catch our flight back to Montana so I could be certain we would leave before dark. It may seem extreme, but I'm paranoid as it is, and Diddy's energy on his voice messages was always so intense that I could only imagine what he'd be like in person.

We arrived to the Malibu home and made our way up the long driveway toward the front door. Before we could knock, we were greeted by an immaculately dressed man holding a tray of fancy cucumber-lemon-mint water. Stinje and I locked eyes. We held up our water bottles and said we were good before being led into the backyard, where we were greeted by a giant infinity pool overlooking a stunning view of the Pacific Ocean illuminated by the midday sun. The sharp-dressed man told us to grab a seat and that Diddy would be down in just a moment. In typical celebrity mind-game fashion, we sat there waiting until he finally came down. During that time I think we had to turn down three or four more fancy drinks. After forty-five minutes, Diddy emerged, arguing with somebody on FaceTime on his phone. I was nervous as Diddy approached. We shook hands and sat down at a marble table. I put my water bottle on the ground right beside my Air Force 1s as one of Diddy's staff asked if Stinje could go and wait inside the house.

In person, Diddy was far more chill than on the phone. His energy was smooth—too smooth—and he listened far more than he talked. He was asking tons of questions about the business and what investing in a company like Cookies would look like. I got bad vibes right away. He seemed snakey and manipulative and was overly accommodating, like a hype man; I know a car salesman when I see one. I've been around pimps my whole life.

As the meeting wrapped, I agreed to let his analyst connect with me and take a look at some numbers to get a better sense of the business. Diddy got his private chef to cook us a nice baked chicken with wine sauce served over a cloud of bulgur and invited Stinje back to the table. Before the clock struck four we were on our way back to the airport.

His analyst ended up reaching out to our team shortly after to dive into the business financials. I'd made it clear before that Cookies was not raising capital at this time, but our fund 12/12 Ventures, which had a large position in Cookies, was. So Diddy couldn't invest directly into Cookies but instead would have to invest into 12/12, if he wanted to get in as an investor. I'm a general partner of the fund, which was established by Parker, myself, and my business partner, Matt Barron. The purpose of the fund was to back businesses that are aligned with Cookies, but it also serves as a vehicle in case our traditional investors ever decided to pull funding—which, spoiler alert, happened. The way I see it, it's one thing to own a business, but you're on a whole other level if you can own the fund that supports the business as well. With 12/12, I also add "fund manager" to my growing list of titles; the growth and the grind never stop.

Eventually, frustrated by the roadblocks we were putting up and the whole process, Diddy asked if he could just acquire Cookies, the entire brand and business. When I said no, he got extremely upset and asked if it was a race thing. Funny thing is, after all that energy and time spent analyzing the financials, he ended up asking for 10 percent of the company in exchange for being a brand ambassador, which I suspected from the beginning was what would happen. That's typical of celebrities. A few months later, Diddy attempted the same move with my rolling paper company, Vibes. When that proved unsuccessful, too, he unfollowed me on Instagram, and I never heard from him again. Another bullet dodged.

Given the recent allegations, it's safe to say it would have been the end of Cookies if Diddy had been brought on board.

Diddy wasn't the only celebrity catch I had conversations with about joining forces. Soon after my meeting with Diddy, I got a Zoom call from Jay-Z. He was attempting to make major waves in the cannabis industry but didn't know the space very well. He ended up launching a cannabis company called Monogram. They sold $100 pre-rolls and had some of the worst packaging and disconnected marketing I've ever seen. Their bud was sold in all-black packages that didn't tell you anything about the strain, nothing about the quality or origin of the bud. They bought an outdoor farm for $17 million, with no plans of extraction, no mixed-light or indoor grow capabilities to create a better growing environment. None of that. Just hella outdoor. They were so green that they were even sending samples to people around the country via FedEx and having people open their gift packages right out of the good ol' FedEx box online, which is straight-up illegal, but they didn't know any better. Worst of all, the joints were terrible. Monogram didn't last long. I remember the industry reacting to his launch, and let's just say it was not positive at all.

As Jay-Z was getting Monogram off the ground, I had a Zoom call with him. He wanted to know about our company, what we were doing that was working and what a future might look like if he were involved. I took the call on my computer in my office and was immediately taken aback by his video background, which was this enormous, beautiful L.A. estate that was so picture-perfect I thought it had to be fake. He was the complete opposite of Diddy. He was cool as fuck. Smooth, but in a real way, not aggressive in the least, and he carried an aura with him that just screamed "success." Who didn't grow up idolizing "Hova" and the way he spread his wings outside of the music space? Needless to say, he was one of my role models, and I told him that as we touched on fashion, alcohol, and other things outside of music. I knew that, deep down, Cookies was on a whole other level from the boutique approach he was trying to achieve with cannabis, but to say that I didn't seriously consider doing something with him would be a total lie. I mean, c'mon, it's Jay-Z. And that's the danger of celebrity. He talked about acquiring the majority of Cookies with stock and some cash. "Listen, I'm going to be the biggest in this space," he told me. "I just think I can get there a lot faster with you. I think this could be big." Ultimately I had to break it to him that I wasn't looking to merge or sell my company just yet. Instead I tossed around an idea on a joint venture that would embrace the Black and Brown communities, empower some new brands, and do a huge social equity campaign. I proudly told him about Cookies U, a cannabis training program I had started for historically marginalized people and those negatively impacted by the War on Drugs.

The idea for Cookies U first came about in 2019 when I was doing a press run for one of my albums. I made appearances on platforms I'd waited my whole career to be on, like *The Breakfast Club* and HOT 97. Instead of talking about my album, I chose to highlight social equity. Where legalization was taking place, many states were recognizing those who had been impacted by the War on Drugs before legalization. In many cases, minorities were most heavily impacted and were rightfully given the first chance to qualify for cannabis licenses, whether in cultivation or storefronts. It was a good idea on paper, but the system was broken. It costs so much money and takes so much knowledge about compliance laws and whatnot to get a cultivation operation or retail storefront up and running. There are massive barriers to entry and no real program in place to educate people on the cannabis space. I noticed a trend with some of the major MSOs and big-money players paying pennies on the dollar to social equity applicants asking them to give up their licenses, which bothered me like crazy. For these start-up minority stakeholders, the money probably felt like a come-up, but what I saw was people selling themselves short without realizing it. There were opportunities for minorities, but the resources were lacking. So I decided to do something about it.

When I'm meeting with investors and other owners in the cannabis industry, I look around these boardrooms and don't see many people that look like me. When we opened our retail stores in San Francisco and New York City, we treated it as a social equity store and made sure we put people from marginalized communities that had been unfairly impacted from before the days of legalization in charge. But it wasn't enough. In any industry, knowledge is key. Preaching online or on the radio is cool, but I knew we needed to do more. As a minority-owned company, we wanted to do something from the heart and use our knowledge to help put more minorities in a position to succeed in cannabis. Parker had developed his farm in Humboldt County, called One Log, and built out the property over the years. We have a storefront, a nursery, a full-term grow operation, a mixed-light greenhouse, a packaging area, genetic testing labs, and so much more. It's a one-stop shop for everything you need to breed, develop, brand, package, and sell cannabis. In other words, the perfect place to teach. So we created Cookies U.

With the help of Cookies' head of social impact, Amanda Friedman, and Jonah Carrington, we designed a program for up to ten social equity students. We even ordered ten tiny homes as student housing and brought them to the property. The students would live at our facility for free, and we even promised to take care of their bills back home for the two-month duration of the program. We put out the word and asked interested applicants to submit a video of why they wanted to join the program and why they should be chosen. We received over ten thousand applications, which let me know how incredibly necessary a program like this was. My goal has always been for our students to pick up enough game and passion to start their own brand. When students graduate, I tell them all the same thing: They are family now. That's what the plant does. It unites and elevates people, and it's why I'm still in the game today. The current manager at our store in New York City, Culture House, is a graduate of Cookies U.

I explained to Jay-Z that we could expand this program to other markets and emphasized that, as an industry, we had to do our best to diversify and that I truly hoped others would open the doors to their platform to help educate. It's more valuable than money. He agreed.

I appreciated Jay-Z reaching out and also the advice he gave me to keep your children and family involved in business. He explained how, before he exited some ventures, he would find a way to make sure his kids had a role in the company once they got older, so they could be a part of the future of those companies. I wish we could have done something together. Jay-Z's brand no longer exists in the cannabis space. If I had been starstruck and reached a deal with him to acquire Cookies, my company probably would have had the same fate as Monogram.

When you have motion, you become magnetic and will inevitably attract all different walks of life, some of whose success can be used as a tactic to get a piece of your company without adding any real value beyond the "wow" factor of having that person as a partner. When talking to venture capitalists or celebrities looking to get a foot into your market, you must understand exactly what they can bring to the table as well as what liability they may bring.

Follow your gut, and you'll know when is the right time to bring in capital or exit your company. A billion and a half dollars later, I'm still not considering an exit. If my twenty-plus years in business has taught me anything, it's how to read people and situations. Never be afraid to throw back even the biggest fish in the ocean.

Chapter 9

SELLING SOAP A THOUSAND WAYS

I've always had a good eye and a special touch when it comes to marketing. I think it's fair to say that I'm addicted to the game. Birthing a brand and building something from the ground up is a high better than any herb I've smoked. Doing it in a way that truly resonates with people. . . . That's *what I live for.*

It's been the biggest blessing and is a total rush—but it's not easy. My work ethic is pretty insane. It has to be. Between the clothing, music, rolling papers, weed, and new brands and ventures, there's so much on my plate that the work never stops. From the moment I wake up until the time I go to bed, I'm on my phone making plays. The running joke among my boys is that when I say, "Alright, this is the last call," everyone laughs and rolls their eyes because we all know damn well it never is. Just the other day, on a two-hour drive from the Cookies headquarters to a legal hearing in Humboldt County, I was chilling in the back seat on back-to-back-to-back-to-back-to-back calls the entire ride.

"Is it always *like this?" asked one of my boys who was riding*

with me, between calls. Before I could answer, the phone rang. I just grinned as I picked it up. Yeah, man. It is.

On top of being the face of my businesses, I've taken the reins with creative directing and marketing. I've never been to school for marketing. Never taken any classes on the subject. I've just worked closely with consumers my entire life and have a strong understanding of what catches people's eye. I've soaked up game from some of the biggest players in history and drawn from my own experience to create a marketing master plan that has seen Cookies become a recognized industry-leading marketer and advertiser. I've mastered the organic way to both seed and launch new brands and products. It's not rocket science. But boy, it does work.

. . .

When you roll it up and smoke it, my marketing philosophy is simple. **Make things feel as real and true to you as possible and introduce it in a way that sticks with your customers.** Never make your marketing feel forced or cheesy. With that mindset, you have a foundation to build upon. From there, a ton of factors come into play, from packaging and branding to social media and creating content to, finally, rolling the product out.

I'll never forget a conversation I had with Peter Karpas, the former chief marketing officer and SVP of Intuit, who also worked at places like PayPal and Procter & Gamble. He was working with us informally during the early days at Cookies, and I loved hearing about his experiences. One afternoon we were talking about different approaches and philosophies to marketing, and he began telling me about his time at P&G working on campaigns for Tide laundry detergent. All laundry soap is basically the same, he explained, and his job was to change little details on the packaging so they could flood the shelf with their product. "My task," he said, "was to sell soap a hundred different ways." That line floored me. It helped me realize how important packaging is.

If you look at the New York market today, for example, even the black market, everyone is selling the same strains—Lemon, Cherry, or Gelato. Everyone is selling the same bud, just with different packaging. So it goes back to what Peter said. People get creative with packaging or oddly enough now put a toy or sticker in with their eighths to differentiate. It's the same thing for people who buy white-label bulk—you're going to have to figure out a way to sell the same thing a hundred different ways.

Back in the days of Sour Diesel and OG Kush, everyone was selling the same shit, but there wasn't any packaging then. Things are different today. Nowadays it's become a packaging contest. It doesn't apply to us specifically because we create new, proprietary genetics, and we stand on that. But in the industry today, in the white or the black market, Peter's insight is extremely relevant to what's going on.

Everybody wants to be the next Cookies. But before you introduce a product and create hype around it, you have to consider what's sitting on the shelves today. Earlier we talked about how packaging impacts the look and feel of your brand. I mentioned the process behind creating my rolling paper company, Vibes, and when I am designing new products or businesses, marketing is always top of mind. Vibes exists in such a saturated—and monopolized—rolling paper market. The bold Vibes logo and gold foil helped us stand out and set a standard and distinguish us from the competition, which is part of the story we wanted to tell consumers. Sure enough, other rolling paper companies started using foil in their packaging. As always, I took it as a compliment. To come in and disrupt an industry that existed way before you and change market trends for packaging—that's something to be proud of.

Remember how, when we first put Girl Scout Cookies out into the world and it blew up in popularity, we began to see knockoff versions of it everywhere after the genetics leaked? I would hear it all the time . . . "Yeah, but is it *really* GSC?" We needed a way to let people know what they were getting was legit, so we began branding our retail bags. The "C" on the bag was more than just a simple and classic way to gain exposure; it was a stamp of validation for our customers. If you weren't getting your weed in these bags, then it wasn't legit Cookies.

I also knew that if people were to start taking pictures of the bags—or better yet, pictures of our bud sitting on top of the bag—that shit would go viral. Instagram has since put on some wild regulations on what you can post, but when we were first getting Cookies off the ground, my feed was absolutely flooded with people posting pictures and videos of Gelato 41 on a Cookies bag, and we generated a ton of buzz off of that. With that "C" bag our product became "Instagrammable," and you can't put a price on that. Like it or not, it makes a difference in how people perceive your product.

Authenticity is essential to marketing. I don't think there is anything worse than forced promotion. Nowhere is this more evident to me than when it comes to paid influencers and celebrity endorsements. I can see a paid influencer campaign from a mile away, and that is a huge turnoff for me as both a consumer and a marketer. But if it's done right, it can be effective. There is an art to it. The goal is always to introduce your product to endorsers or influencers as organically as possible. If you can make a celebrity fall in love with your product, like the rappers who fell in love with Girl Scout Cookies and Cherry Pie, then you are on your way to winning.

But I'm always seeing brand owners drop the ball when it comes to celebrity endorsements. They'll show up backstage at a concert and give an influential rapper a pound baggie of some mass-produced shit, take a picture with them, and think it's going to prop their brand up. The artist, meanwhile, is going to feel used. Maybe they smoke a little bit, but I bet you they just end up giving it away to most of their friends and never thinking about it again. I've seen it happen a bunch. Same with streetwear—if you give someone a box of clothes, they might keep one shirt and give the rest to their friends. That's not the player way to do it. Put your product directly in an influential person's hands if you really want to create genuine hype around it.

If you are paying, sure, now there's a celeb in a picture holding your product, but at the same time you just became a trick to them. It's just like in a strip club, when you're the one tipping the girl, you're always going to be the trick. If you're paying someone to promote your product, will they still continue to promote it once you stop paying them? Of course not. Remember that if you do a typical paid influencer campaign, their love for your brand stops the moment the checks stop. I can do more with a few grams of brand-new bud in a sandwich bag than any paid influencer campaign.

Fact is, people love a story attached to a brand, and they love to have something before everyone else. It's especially true of celebrities. If I see artists, I'll go up to them and give them a couple buds in a clear bag. Even if I have a pound or a few pounds, I'll just share a few buds to make it feel scarce or limited. You never see luxury brands like Louis Vuitton, Gucci, or Hermès give away product for free, and that's why rappers boast about it. It's a flex to have it. Why wouldn't I treat my brand the same way? At the end of the day, nobody wants mass-produced, highly available *anything*. They want what the next man can't get, and that goes for clothing, alcohol, shoes, tables at trendy restaurants, and definitely weed.

So I'll approach an artist or influencer and explain, "This is some new shit we're working on. Try it out, let me know how you like it." I hype it up and smoke it with them. From there, they feel juiced, like they have access to something super exclusive. If they choose to hype up your product and let their fans know about it, it will be because they want to, not because you paid them to. Believe me, consumers can tell the difference.

For example, we have a licensing deal with cannabis retailer LooseLeaf, and I'm pretty sure Travis Scott only smokes our Cookies & Cream from LooseLeaf. I've never talked to the guy about it, never brought up the idea of him promoting it. But I know it's all he smokes. The kind of goodwill we get from him using our product, the shots of our packaging backstage at his concerts, and people seeing him voluntarily using our product . . . That shit is *priceless*.

For my streetwear, for Cookies clothing, I never gifted artists clothes. I would wait until they asked me, and at that point the exchange would be done with purpose. If they're excited about it, they're going to want to tell people about it. Pretty soon you'll find the wheels moving on a marketing machine that you don't need to steer from behind the wheel. Take the original Cookies store on Melrose in Hollywood. There was a clothing store beside it that allowed us to stock Cookies shirts and sweaters. When artists, influencers, or athletes came through to get some weed, they would naturally head next door to check out the clothes, too. All of a sudden they're coming out wearing Cookies gear, which made the weed even hotter. It was a cycle. Everything complemented each other. But my point is that it was all natural and organic—if you force something down someone's throat, they're never going to want it.

. . .

Now let's get into content. The saying is true: Content is king. Bill Gates was the first person to mention that phrase, in the mid-1990s. Today it's *everything*. But how do you go about making it? For starters: Document everything.

YouTube was the perfect platform to post what I call mini-documentaries, ten-minute videos that document damn near every step of the way in the building of Cookies. Go on YouTube, search "Berner" or "Berner Bigger Business," and you'll find videos of me back in the day printing up the first wave of Cookies gear, pulling red strings through the hoodies, and packing and shipping orders. I was just beginning to get the company off the ground, and I wanted to bring fans along on that journey. Not only does it help to tell your story when you succeed, but naturally it also builds a community of fans that leaves people attached to your brand. They know it's authentic and that your heart is in it. You'd be surprised how much pride people take in supporting you from the very beginning. Take them on that journey with you. Not only will you build your customer base, but your content will organically expose them to your brand and products. Companies like Apple, Nike, and Supreme have turned this into an art form and have built wildly loyal customer bases in the process.

Twitter—now "X"—is like my public diary, letting fans know what I'm feeling or thinking at any given time; I see Instagram as a powerful way to *show* people what I'm doing—showcasing the products I'm developing and taking them behind the scenes for that process.

I grew audiences of millions on all these platforms. They were a way for me to show people who I am and what I'm about. But they also helped me to reach new fans.

So much content I see today is dry and lacks creativity. Professional product shots or models showing off your brand get tired and repetitive. Instead, **show them how your product is made, the process behind it, and by the time it's released, they'll be thirsty for it.** It's a perfect strategy for an industry like cannabis. Any new grower should be making a video of themselves and the homies pollinating and breeding a new strain. Show people the vegetation process and the beauty of the buds sprouting on the flowing vines. Bring them into the dry room where the plants are hanging, and then show them what the finished dry flower looks like. Take them inside your packaging and design process, and then finally put up a post letting customers know that the bud is available now. By the time it hits the market, the consumer has already seen and heard about the product eight times before they've even had a chance to buy it. That's how you get as many eyes as possible without the need for a multimillion-dollar ad campaign.

As easy as it is to get wrapped up in the creation and promotion of your product, don't forget how effective social media can be in the rollout. Here's an example: If I have a show in L.A., I will create a social media post saying something like, "I want to do a show in L.A. What venue should I book?" That starts a conversation (even though those details are already locked in). Then I'll do a follow-up post promoting the date ("Will you be there on April 8th, Los Angeles?"). After that, I'll post a recap video or another piece of original content showing the last few times I performed in the city to remind people of what a good time they had—or could have had. Finally, after building up all that hype, I'll post the flyer with all the concert details and watch as the tickets get snatched up right away. This works really well, especially when the product is a limited drop or limited-ticket event. Go ahead and create that FOMO. That'll push your customers to make a move. When it comes to staying ahead of the algorithm and maximizing your potential on social media, the key is to listen to the kids. The youth are the gateway to what's trending and what's working today. The future of social media is limitless. It's taken over traditional marketing, and these days a brand is going to run an ad with a TikToker before they put up a billboard.

Ultimately, the rollout technique allows for engagement, which should be one of your biggest goals on social media. You want your supporters and customers talking in your comments. Even better, you want them talking *to you*. Insert yourself in the conversation and make people feel included, involved, and invested in your business. It helps build a community and is a powerful demonstration that people care about what you have going on. You'll see plenty of artists, brands, and influencers post and ghost. Not me. I'm hella active in my comment section, vibing with fans and creating conversations. It's Marketing 101, baby. The more people talking about a product drop, the better.

. . .

One of the most impactful ways to build interest in your product and get more hype and eyes on it is through collaborations. I've been a part of some of the sickest collabs in music, clothing, and weed spaces and have figured out the art of a strong brand partnership. A well-designed and carefully packaged collaboration will get the fans of the collaborating partner juiced and could bring your brand to new audiences and markets.

I learned a lot coming up in the rap game. Features on tracks and working the group album hustle had me working heavily with other artists. The more material I put out with other artists, the more I was able to get myself in front of more eyes and grab different fan bases. I figured it was only natural to apply the same strategy while building CookiesSF. We've done legendary collaborations with our clothing, and it keeps the brand exciting, relevant, and fresh.

In fact, we've been doing it from the very beginning. Day One followers out there will remember our very first collabs—one that the collaborator didn't even know about. In the music video for "Yoko," when the world saw the Cookies wordmark for the first time on the front of my hoodie, I wore another Cookies sweater at the end of the video with C-O-O-K-I-E-S written across it in red. In place of the two O's was the iconic Rolling Stones tongue logo with a pair of round cookies on the tongue. It became one of our most popular designs out the gate and a bestseller for a few years. At the beginning, our brand wasn't big enough for the Stones—or the company that owns and manages their licensing—to notice. Once they did notice, they sued us. More than anything, I felt like it was a huge compliment to us that we were even on their radar.

I asked if we can just use the logo and pay a royalty. "Fuck, no," I was told by the company. "You guys are *done*."

At that point we had to take care of business and ended up paying six figures in damages, but it meant that we were poppin'.

Five years later, I asked our licensing guy to reach out to the company again. "I bet you the same people who told us no five years ago don't even work there anymore," I said. Turns out I was right. By the time we reached back out to them, our brand had grown. When they did their due diligence with us they found an established streetwear brand with a loyal following, and we ended up getting a license and brought back the original red wordmark shirt from the "Yoko" video along with a bunch of new designs. And those shirts did crazy sales. The Rolling Stones gear was a throwback for our earliest customers who kept asking us whatever happened to that look, and it was a dope collection for new customers, too.

I really do believe that powerful collaborations in the clothing space have played a big role in Cookies being a household name today. **You have to do things that complement and fit your brand.** One collab that pulled that off extremely well for us was our relationship with Starter. When we learned that Starter's license had become available, we jumped on it. Starter is a big brand and represents the culture. You've got to remember that back in the day they were so popular that people would get robbed for their Starter jackets. I remember I used to see stories about it on the news. But *Cookies* and Starter? *Berner* and Starter? That's even bigger, and the hype reaction from people who were juiced to find out that Cookies had a Starter jacket was cool to see. It was a natural fit. Starter brings a nostalgia vibe that we knew our urban base would love, and they ate it up. We rolled the Starter jackets the same way we do most collabs: We make a limited release for the product online that sells out very fast (we sold out every SKU of the first release in a minute). After that, when the demand is at its peak, we do a bigger wholesale order with different colorways. Our fans emptied the racks when those jackets came out.

Another big collab was with the restaurant chain White Castle. In 2022, we put out a clothing capsule just in time for 4/20 but with a twist: If you came into a White Castle franchise on 4/20 you were given access to a secret menu. All you had to do was mention Cookies. It was a win-win, which all good collabs should be. We had the buzz and could bring people through their doors. They had the legitimacy of a fast-food chain, which for a clothing brand like Cookies that was so intertwined with cannabis was a big fucking deal. When looking for a collab partner, it's important to find someone who can bring value to your brand. But for a company like Cookies making a name for itself in an emerging industry, **it's also crucial to find partners who can help normalize your brand by associating it with traditional business.**

Currently, we're designing one of our most epic collabs yet: a collection with the Grateful Dead. Growing up where I'm from, you couldn't escape the Dead. They were Haight Street. They were the flower movement, the hippie movement, the peace movement. They were the voices of that whole generation and San Francisco culture at its finest. I grew up with murals of Jerry Garcia all over the city and seeing stickers with the iconic dancing bear logo—the "Jerry Bear"—all over everything, everywhere. The Grateful Dead set the tone for what a true cult following looks and feels like and have been a model for how to build a dedicated following. I look at the Cookies "C" as an equivalent to the Jerry Bear.

In a time before mine, they were the Cookies of their era. That's why, when the opportunity came up to work with the Dead, I knew it was a very big moment in my career. It all began six or seven years back, when a mutual friend connected me with Bob Weir, guitarist, vocalist, and one of the founders of the Grateful Dead.

I met Bobby at his rehearsal space, this industrial building in a business park in Marin, California. From the moment you step through the doors you can't help but notice the Dead memorabilia *everywhere*. On one wall was a giant mural of Jerry Garcia's face. I walked toward it, and as I got closer I realized that it was made up entirely of hotel keys and sleeves saved up from the decades of touring.

Bobby was there jamming with his band, Wolf Bros, featuring Don Was on bass and Jay Lane on drums. I watched them jam out a bit and was in awe of their sound setup, featuring all these tricked-out speakers hanging from the ceiling. With those speakers, they could make the room sound like they were in any location—an outdoor amphitheater, a small club, a garage, a recording studio, the bottom of a well, you name it. It was the craziest sound design I've ever seen. When they wrapped up, Bobby made his way over to me to say hello. His gray-white hair hung over his eyes, and he had a great big beard with a bushy moustache. He was very brotherly and welcoming but very quiet. I felt a great wisdom coming from the guy. You could tell he'd been around the world and has seen it all. He seemed to like me and my energy and the fact that I was from San Francisco. Fact is, there's not a lot of us who make big waves—cultural waves—coming out of the Bay Area. Cookies is a cultural wave, and he understood that. Bobby was treating me like SF royalty and introducing me to the band, and we were all vibing. A cool experience, and I left it at that.

We stayed in touch, and a year or so later, in February of 2021, Bobby reached out and asked me to perform a song with him and the Wolf Bros during a live virtual St. Patrick's Day concert they were putting on. This was during the Covid era. I was pretty nervous and didn't know how one of my songs would resonate with their audience, but Bobby told me not to worry about it and that he had it all figured out.

I arrived at the Wolf Bros compound the day before the concert to go over everything and rehearse. The idea was that I would rap on one of their existing songs, and the boys began tossing around ideas on which record would feel best and landed on an old Grateful Dead song called "Liberty." Typically after I first hear a beat, it takes me an hour or so to write lyrics, so I wasn't too worried about it. I listened to "Liberty" a few times and went home with an idea of what I wanted to do and say.

The next morning, I came back to the compound for the show, which took place in the jam space in front of a wall of screens filled with a virtual audience watching from home. The band had such a great energy and made me feel like family. I had some lyrics written out from the day before. With a huge smile on my face as I shared the stage with Bobby, I watched as he counted in the band to start up "Liberty." After just a few notes, he stopped the band and said he wanted to slow down the BPM big time—almost by half. They started up the tune again. When it came time for me to rap, nothing was working. The words didn't fit. I had written a flow for the faster beat and what I wrote seemed impossible over this slower BPM. I was hella embarrassed, messing up in front of Bobby and told the band that I would figure it out during a break before the live show began.

My brother Jay Lane must have sensed my nervousness, and he quickly recorded a loop of the new beat on his practice drums and sent it to me. I pulled it up on my phone and, just minutes before we went live, I dialed in, rewrote my parts, and figured it out. Showtime.

"In some circles, he needs no introduction," Bobby said as I walked onto the stage and faced the wall of people on the screen—and none of 'em looked anything like me. I think it's the most nervous I've ever been to perform! But I came out of the gate hot and crushed it.

I'm the rap game Jerry
My stat game crazy

Frisco City, born in the late '80s
I hate COVID; let's get high and make babies.

Man, I ain't seen y'all in a year
My little girl called, said, "Dad you're all I hear"
The shrooms kicked in, it's getting hard to steer
Did the world ever think they'd see Berner and Bobby Weir?

I pointed to Bobby, who was standing directly to my right, and the virtual fans started cheering as he stepped to the mic to sing the chorus.

The gig was a success, and I had planted a seed with his fans and mine. I don't like to discuss business with people I'm becoming friends with, so Bob and I never discussed a formal collab between Cookies and the Dead, even though it was on my mind. We remained friends and, many years later, I had someone on my team reach out to the people who hold the licenses for the Grateful Dead, who agreed to work with us. And I know it only worked out because of that virtual gig and the natural friendship that blossomed between Bobby and me from there. Now you'll be seeing Cookies backpacks, hats, rolling trays, and all sorts of accessories and clothing featuring the Dead's iconic imagery on our gear. After we closed the deal, Bobby's manager reached out all excited and told me he was proud of us for making it happen, because the Dead's license is famously *not* easy to get. The whole process, years in the making, was organic and made sense for the brand.

Of course, we love to do things that people aren't expecting as well, and every now and then a licensing opportunity comes about with a movie like *Scarface, Child's Play* (Chucky), or my all-time favorite, *Goodfellas*. I'm always looking for things that can help us stand out from the crowd. A lot of cannabis companies are trying to get into clothing now, and that's cool—everyone is free to jump into our lane—but I need to make sure we're always doing it better.

I remember one year when Black Friday was approaching, I had the idea to hold "Trap Friday" on the Cookies website. Everyone sells discounted clothes on Black Friday, but what if we could release something new on that day? I wondered if we could compete with the discounted items, and it became a challenge to myself.

Back then, the rapper Gucci Mane, a.k.a. "Trap God," was finishing up a stint in jail, and I reached out to him through some connections in the streets (let's just say I know people who know people). I proposed the idea of a Cookies x Trap God collab and said that shit would really pop off if he wrote a handwritten letter from prison talking to his fans. We would release the letter on our social media channels just before the clothing drops, and the hype would be massive, I explained. He said he was down, and he wrote up his letter and sent it to me. We released the letter on Black Friday and announced the clothing partnership. That day, the Trap God clothing capsule outsold the entire Black Friday sales on our website—which was 50 percent off on everything storewide. We learned a lot about our brand through that collab, because it showed that despite a major sale on popular items, what the people really want is the *new* shit.

Well-marketed collaborations have helped elevate Cookies in the weed space as well—and not just celebrity collabs, though we'll get to those in a minute.

At Cookies we embraced the talented breeders out there early on. It's one thing to collab with famous people, but to uplift and shine light on those in the field breeding and curating incredible flavors has been super rewarding. Those collabs began out of necessity. Back when it was time to transition to the legal market, we as a crew weren't organized. We were still growing in people's houses and didn't always have the long play in mind. So, as always, I had to get creative. Many of the breeders I wanted to work with had been thriving in the gray legacy market but lacked a presence in the legal market. With the megaphone we had thanks to social media, my thought was that we were in a unique position to help breeders build their brands. In turn, they could help grow and supply product at the scale that we needed and continue to fill our bags with the best weed out there. It was a win-win, which you'll find is at the heart of the best collaborations. We formed partnerships with select breeders and helped build and manage their brands, taking them around the world with us, one shelf at a time. In some cases these collabs were limited one-offs and built on very straightforward royalty agreements, and we include the breeder's logo on our packaging to help expose them to new customers. The push from myself and the Cookies brand can take a breeder or company to a whole other level. It's a really dope trade of services.

One of my favorite breeder partnerships in the last few years has actually been with my original Cookie Fam member, Kenny Powerz, and his brand, Powerzzzup. I helped design the wordmark logo, which resembles the Golden Gate Bridge because I wanted it to scream San Francisco, and I turned him on to social media and began doing a bunch of content with him. Like I've said, even though things didn't play out with the crew after the fallout from The Group, I still had their backs and never closed the door on working with them again as the Cookies empire expanded. In 2019, Kenny and I went on Instagram live from the basement of a small grow house in San Francisco to sample a bunch of different crossbreeds he had been cooking up in the lab. All the different strains were in jars, each labeled with a different number. One of the strains—jar number 20—stood out from the rest, and as we were smoking he showed off the jar in front of the camera, saying, "This that number 20, that Gary Payton." He just sort of blurted it out, and I didn't even really take in what he said. We just moved on to the other flavors as the livestream continued. It would be months before any of the weed we were sampling would hit the market, but I loved giving fans a look behind the scenes of the R&D process. We ended up selecting the number 20 jar to move forward with production, and I gave the strain a new name: Snow Montana.

Bootlegging is so common in our industry that in just a matter of weeks, people started spotting bootlegged Cookies bags with "Gary Payton" on them. Before you knew it, they were flooding the Bay Area streets—and all just from a throwaway comment made on an IG story. *That's* the kind of juice we have. Mind you, I wasn't aware that this was happening until a few weeks later when I got a phone call from my brother, Matt, who had heard through some connections that Gary Payton, the real-life person, wanted to have a sit-down with me in Oakland. I never followed sports, so I was only a little embarrassed to admit that I didn't know who Payton was. I phoned up Kenny. "Yo, who is Gary?" I asked. He laughed and said he couldn't believe I didn't know who he was. He explained that Gary Payton is a retired NBA superstar from Oakland and a legend coming out of the Bay Area who wore jersey no. 20 while playing for the Seattle SuperSonics in the '90s. Kenny is a huge sports fan, and it was probably the first thing that came to his mind when he saw the number on that jar. So I set up the meeting.

I crossed the bridge from San Francisco and pulled up to an empty Oakland restaurant where I was supposed to meet Gary. After a little while, he pulled up in a white Range Rover, alone, like a real one. He hopped out of the car and shook my hand, his face expressionless, all business. There was a long awkward silence as we sat down at the table, two legends from completely different worlds. After a few minutes, he reached into his pocket and pulled out a bag and dropped it onto the table. "What's this?" he asked, as we both looked down at a crinkled, terribly designed baggie featuring an oversized jersey with the number 20 on it and the name "Gary Payton" written across the top. In the bottom corner was the Cookies logo. He told me he heard that I'd been releasing weed with his name on it and not paying him for it. He was pissed. The more he spoke, the angrier he got. I tried to pour ice on the situation and told him that I'd never seen that bag before and explained that it was a bootleg. I pulled out a bag of our London Pound Cake 75 and showed it to him. The design was crisp and professional, and the bag was soft-touch Mylar and felt great, not like the dollar-store packaging on the bootleg bag. I opened the bag Gary had brought with him and stuck my nose inside. I took a whiff and just laughed. It was just a lemon cherry strain, and a weak batch at that. That's when it clicked and I remembered Kenny shouting out "Gary Payton" on Instagram. I explained the situation to Gary, told him that our strain was actually called Snow Montana. Then I mentioned how if Cookies *did* have a strain called "Gary Payton" that I would do it big and create something dope and timeless, like a Wheaties box.

He leaned forward in his chair. It was like the conversation had switched gears on a dime and now suddenly we were getting amped about doing something together. "Well, let me see that number 20, then," he said. He wanted to give some to his son. "Let Little Gary try it and see if it's the truth."

I left the meeting and called Kenny and we got a sample out to Gary. About a week later, Gary called me up. "Little Gary loved it," he told me. I wasn't surprised. Of course he did. It was fuckin' fire. Gary and I started talking about what a partnership between us would look like—but there was a catch: The Snow Montana strain belonged to Kenny, and the royalties were supposed to go to him. I had to convince Kenny to officially rename the strain Gary Payton—which he was cool with—and to split his royalties with Gary—which Kenny was hella opposed to, at first. Let's say the strain makes $200. Whatever the profits, Cookies would take half, and the other half would go to Gary and Kenny to split two ways. I was persistent and explained the opportunity and Kenny began to realize the value that a collaboration like this could bring. Before the year was out, the Gary Payton strain quickly became one of the most popular in America and one of our bestsellers. We were the first brand to name a strain after a basketball player and put their face on the baggy. It was a three-way collab between a breeder, celebrity, and our brand.

For the most part, celebrity or artist collabs in the weed space don't work. But our collaborations are based on organic relationships and high-quality products. It's a recipe many cannabis brands have tried to mimic but have failed.

Just like with clothing, cannabis collabs can be a great way to breathe new life into a brand. Take our 2023 collab with singer-songwriter Erykah Badu, for example. I'd met Erykah four years earlier and talked about putting out a Cookies strain together. We called it "That Badu." She liked the idea but wasn't quite ready, and we stayed in touch through a mutual friend. When she told me she was finally ready, we made sure to take the time to do it right. Erykah has a huge cult following and is extremely hands-on and creative, so I knew the potential to do something special was there. As we discussed plans for "That Badu," a Cookies line of flower and products that included teas, creams, and gummies, I was impressed by how in tune with her fans she was. We took our time not just choosing genetics but also designing the brand's look and feel. Erykah is probably the most hands-on person other than myself that I've ever collaborated with. Her close involvement is a big part of what made the collab a success.

We linked up in L.A. and documented the whole process, filming it for our blog. The first time the public saw Erykah smoke was with me. Those kinds of moments help our fan bases feel like they are part of the journey and show people that the passion is there on both sides. To launch the product, we set up a bunch of meet-and-greet sessions, and it was so cool to see Erykah with her fan base. She would take the time to meet every single person, even if it meant being there for four, five, six hours. That kind of dedication is rarer than you'd think. I didn't know that her fans would be fans of mine, and vice versa. She has a hippie audience, and they love bud, which I didn't know before we began working together. It's been a great partnership. I've been able to build with Erykah, and it's been an amazing journey.

Like I learned way back in my earliest days at the Hemp Center, one of the coolest things about weed is that it connects people from all backgrounds. With That Badu I saw a fan base I wouldn't have expected to vibe with me or Cookies jump on board. In fact, there's one collab that was discussed that hasn't been done yet that would prove the power of weed to bring people together. We'll call it "Berner, Bobby, and Badu." Erykah is down. Bobby Weir is down. You know I'm down. We just haven't found the time to do it . . . yet.

Partnerships and collabs with breeders, artists, and celebrities have helped make Cookies a go-to in the space. At the end of the day, these collabs are a marketing play. When done right, they'll let you spread your wings and find ways to get out of your box while reaching new audiences. Through collaborations you will also learn the power of networking and working with people. That in itself is a powerful tool, and it's a skill many people don't naturally have. Of course, it's important to note that I don't work with anyone just because they're famous. I've turned down some of your favorite artists and athletes because I wanted to preserve our brand integrity.

But sometimes a collab is a no-brainer, like the recent *Freak Brothers* cartoon series—a reboot of the cult classic from the '70s called *The Fabulous Furry Freak Brothers,* about three stoner brothers from San Francisco. In the reboot, the brothers smoke some bomb-ass weed that puts them in a coma, and they wake up in the year 2020. The cast is stacked, starring Woody Harrelson, Tiffany Haddish, John Goodman, and Pete Davidson. When I heard about the show, I knew we had to get Cookies involved. I figured, what if the product they smoked in the cartoon was based off a real strain that viewers could go out and grab in stores? So we're bringing the cartoon to life with a dope clothing capsule, *Freak Brothers* grinders and rolling accessories, and a 2.5-gram infused joint called the LSD joint and other cross-promotional products. They even put my character, Berner, in the show, and I did the voice acting. It's a huge step for both myself and the brand. With the cartoon and two *Freak Brothers* movies in the works, it opens new doors and will help continue to make Cookies a household name.

. . .

I never imagined that my genuine love for my brand and the natural ways I used to market it would gain respect from leaders in the marketing world and open doors way beyond cannabis, like getting to meet Jason Deland, a legend in the marketing game.

I got an invite to meet him at his Anomaly headquarters on Hudson Street in Manhattan. As I stepped into the top floor of their gorgeous old limestone building, Deland's work spoke for itself. On the walls were framed mood boards and design templates from iconic campaigns they were behind—Budweiser, Apple, Beats by Dre, so many more. They were on display like in a museum.

Jason came out and greeted me. This was shortly after my *Forbes* cover and when I was making real noise with Cookies, and he'd invited me to meet. There was a notion that we could take him on as an executive and creative director alongside me if we were to go public. Jason was a clean-cut dude with big thick glasses and a leather coat on. His shop was amazing. You could feel the energy in the space. Seeing creatives thrive and kick around ideas while looking at stunning views of the city felt like I was in a dream. Jason pointed to an empty desk by the window. "You see there?" he asked. "That's where Katie Beal Brown used to sit. She was one of our best marketers." He then told the story of how she created a hard seltzer and ended up selling the brand for what I heard rumored was something crazy. She probably got hella game from working with brands like Budweiser and then built up her own and sold it. I thought that was just amazing. I felt like I was in the big leagues. Shit, I *was*.

Jason continued to tour me around the building. There was a maze of hallways, and I was getting a bit disoriented. "This building is kind of a trip," I told him. "Well, yeah," he said. "We bought two buildings and connected them together." *What the fuck!?* I thought. *Well, that's pretty tight.*

We ended up in his office, with floor-to-ceiling windows of the most amazing view of New York City. His assistant brought us lunch and we chopped it up. He was giving me game on his experience working with Apple co-founder and CEO Steve Jobs and all different kinds of companies and campaigns, including several

Super Bowl commercials. I was just blown away by it all. To get props on what I built with Cookies and how I've marketed it from someone like Jason was confirmation that I have a talent in marketing. While we were in the office, he pointed at a letter framed on the wall. It was a speech Steve Jobs had given to Jason and his team while they were creating the famous "Think Different" campaign from the late '90s and early 2000s. While Jobs spoke, Jason transcribed every word he said and framed the speech on his wall. He could tell how drawn I was to it.

At the end of our creative session, he got up and pulled the frame off the wall, wrote a personal note on the back, and handed it to me. "Here, take this with you." I was honored. On the flight home, I read it closely.

"To me, marketing is about values," Jobs begins his speech. "This is a very complicated world, and a very noisy world." He talks about Apple's evolution and the groundwork the company had laid, including the iconic *Nineteen Eighty-Four*–inspired commercial, which, Jobs reminds the room, was "voted the best ad ever made." He explains that he felt the Apple brand had been neglected, that too much time and energy had been spent touting specific technological components of Apple's products. Then he gets to the heart of it, the most important question the company should ask of itself when beginning a marketing campaign, and what all customers inherently want to know:

> *Who is Apple and what is it that we stand for? Where do we fit in this world? What we are about isn't making boxes for people to get their jobs done, although we do that well. Better than almost anybody in some cases. But Apple's about something more than that. . . . Believe me, the products and the distribution strategy and the manu-*

> *facturing are totally different. . . . But core values, those things shouldn't change.*

I still have the speech proudly displayed at my crib.

Being at the table with the likes of Jason and Peter is a great feeling. That shit is empowering, a drug unto itself. And it's the marketing skills I've demonstrated that got me there. I remember speaking at an event for the "Forbes 30 Under 30." There were some pretty big names in attendance, like Kendall Jenner and Bad Bunny, and I was nervous leading up to it. When I arrived they put one of those skinny microphones on my ear, like the ones Jobs wore during his product demos. Once I saw myself with that mic it was like, "Damn, I'm about to do some TED Talk shit." I felt *powerful.* At another event, I spoke in New York to a crowd of educated business professionals about branding in the cannabis industry, knowing that my background couldn't have been more different. But they were there to listen and learn from me. It goes back to when I was working as a bartender at Jelly's. The owner of the bar would always tell me how he never wanted to hire someone out of bartending school. He'd rather hire a former barista like me or someone with practical experience. The same thing applies to marketing. People like people who are hands-on and self-taught over someone fresh out of business school who is more than likely going to apply a textbook approach that just isn't going to help you differentiate.

Never forget that you bring something unique and powerful to the table. If you are in a room where you feel you don't belong, know that you are in that room for a reason. Sometimes charisma, personality, knowledge of specific markets, life experience in places like an urban market can be just as powerful as the education these guys have. You went to Harvard and learned how to apply what you learned in school? Great. Me, I just sold weed and happened to reach a massive demographic a lot of marketers didn't even know about. So I've always understood the value I brought to the table. Understanding your value is so important, and that's why I succeed in corporate settings. What I have is what they don't have, and it's what they want. It's why I do really well in partnerships with corporate people, because I know how to bring a certain kind of charisma and personality that they just don't have. I own that; I'm good at that. They let me do what I do, and I let them do what they do.

At the end of the day, you have to make sure you love your brand or business. Keep it true to who you are so you can put everything you have behind it. Be creative but organic, and figure out how to reach people in a way that not only resonates but makes them feel good. Stamp your logo on everything and recognize that your supporters and followers could—and should—be your biggest marketing asset. Collectively, they'll have more reach than you ever will. Find ways and make time to connect with them. After all, marketing should be fun. Ideas should be shared and brought to life with your friends and collaborators. Understanding human nature and establishing trends will be a game changer for your company. And while not everyone will have to sell soap a hundred different ways, understanding that concept and the process behind it will open your eyes to the true power of reaching people.

420
Hippie Hill
20
20
Forbes
berner
marijuana
meltdown

Chapter 10

BACK-AGAINST-THE-WALL MODE

When it's fight-or-flight mode, I don't run. As a good friend once put it: Back-Against-the-Wall Bernie is a scary thing. There's nothing like some good ol' pressure to motivate you to be at your best, to push your creativity, work ethic, and drive beyond its limits. There have been times when I made huge purchases just so that I could see my bank account balance drop and feel that hunger, which naturally puts my hustle into overdrive.

I think about the days I spent two years ago in a California courtroom when Cookies was in the middle of major litigation and it felt like the fate of my company was on the line. I couldn't help but think where I went wrong. From my seat up against the wall of the small room, filled with about fifteen people, I had a clear view of the back of my lawyer's head. Up on the stand, with arbitrator Hon. David A. Garcia looking on, my partner, Parker, was being cross-examined by the other team's counsel. To my left were the people suing me and my company, smiling at me and even giving me an occasional wink—as if only they knew the eventual out-

come, lol. These are people who I thought respected me and my vision. It was a very strange environment, and a total bummer to be in that place at any time, but especially at this point in my career where I've worked so hard to build my business up—and pulled it off, which only meant that I had more to lose. To make matters worse, the catering was terrible, serving dry, tasteless food. I couldn't wait to leave. Imagine listening to the most absurd lies about yourself for eight or nine hours a day and not being able to say anything in response. Not a word. It's painful.

As my partner, Parker, said in the midst of the battle: "It's time to be sweet to some and strong with others." No matter what comes our way, I have confidence we'll be just fine. I've conquered the largest obstacles life can hand you and made some of my biggest moves while I was down. Whether it be lawsuits, cancer, divorce, or the court of public perception, I've overcome some intense battles. And I still have a few more left to win.

. . .

I am kicking back on the massive sectional couch in the living room of my home in the Bay Area. My dog, Junior, a White Labrador and the coolest, calmest dog you ever met, is chillin' at my side with his head in my lap. Gazing at the view through the giant floor-to-ceiling windows, I feel a wave of calm as the ocean and beautiful mountains in the distance stare back at me. I spark one up and reflect on how good life has been.

It was early 2020, and Cookies was on a wild run. Our stores were opening all over the world, and our brand was expanding globally. And while the Covid-19 pandemic was wreaking havoc, cannabis had been declared "an essential business," which meant that our storefronts remained open—and man, did they boom.

Shit, I thought to myself. *You've got everything you could ever want, bro. . . . What are you missing?* I thought about Mom and her battle with stomach cancer, and the answer popped into my mind. *A private doctor. I need a private doctor to make sure I'm good.* I called up Parker.

"Do you know any private doctors? You know, like some rich, White ones?" He laughed.

"You're fuckin' funny," Parker said. "But I do."

I wanted the extra care and attention. I wanted to be treated like a human being and not a number. But I also had an ulterior motive. There was a lot of talk back then about the drug ivermectin and how it could be used to treat or protect from Covid. I was so goddamn nervous about getting sick, and I really wanted a plug for it. I figured I could get some private doctor to get me on that shit, no questions asked.

Sure enough, Parker mentioned that one of the investors in our Venture Fund ran a concierge doctor's office called Private Medical, where he serviced a very limited number of patients, mostly Silicon Valley tech giants. As always, Parker was looking out for me, and he put in a call.

Dr. Jordan Shlain told Parker that, although his practice was full, as an investor he would be willing to take me on. It was a huge relief. I imagined a patient-doctor relationship where I could call him and ask for anything I needed, and he would provide it. We had an initial consult over the phone, and Dr. Shlain said there would be a $40,000 annual fee to join his practice. And nothing covered by insurance. I mentioned that I wanted a prescription for ivermectin. He shut that shit down immediately and told me absolutely not. *Wait,* I thought, *why am I going to pay this guy a $40,000 per year fee if he won't even hook me up?* I considered how plenty of my rapper friends would blow that kind of money in one night on bottle service at a club and figured for the sake of my health I might as well move forward with the doctor regardless. We set up an in-person visit for later that week.

I arrived at his office on California Street, in a beautiful, swanky neighborhood near Pacific Heights. The office was immaculately clean, and on the walls was an impressive collection of framed vinyl records. Dr. Shlain greeted me in the waiting room and introduced himself as "Doctor J." We went into his office, sat down at a desk, and discussed my health and my weight, and he brought up a series of blood tests he wanted to run. One of them, he said, was brand-new and could screen for upward of fifty different types of cancers through a single blood draw. Sounded good to me. We added it to our list of labs and said our goodbyes. Three weeks later, I was on a call with one of my friends, laughing so hard I thought I'd cracked a rib. That's when I saw the text: *It's Doctor J. Do you have a second to chat?*

I had already received my A1C and other lab tests, which all came back negative. My stomach dropped. I told my friend I had to go, hung up the phone, and collapsed on the living room couch. I watched as my sixteen-year-old daughter grabbed a bottle of yerba mate tea from the fridge and flashed me a contagious smile, the kind that brings dads to their knees. I scrolled through the contacts on my phone and clicked on his name. He picked up before the first ring was finished and got straight to the point. "Gilbert," he said, "your Grail results came back. You have colon cancer."

I was in shock. I was hyperaware because of what happened to Mom. I had had a colonoscopy a few years earlier and was 100 percent in the clear then. No matter, we scheduled a colonoscopy for two weeks out in the hopes that it was just a cancerous polyp that could simply be removed during that procedure. I didn't tell my community online at first, but I told everyone around me that the blood tests were saying I had colon cancer. And then I had no choice but to wait. I couldn't understand why it took so long to book a colonoscopy, and why I couldn't just get one the next day—or even the same day!—but it wasn't an option. I had to wait two weeks. The anxiety leading up to the colonoscopy was unreal, and the feeling of dread and uncertainty lingered in every moment. It was draining. Those two weeks felt like two hundred years.

When it came time for the procedure, I was reassured that I was young—in my early thirties—and that my condition probably wasn't too serious, that they would cut it out and I'd move on with my life. I woke up from the procedure in a daze. Half-awake, I immediately asked the doctor, "Did you cut that shit out?" When she told me that they couldn't, that the tumor was too big and that I needed to schedule an appointment with Doctor J to explore our next options ASAP, I began to cry like a baby. Instantly. Just bawling, like a toddler who had dropped their ice cream cone on the sidewalk.

I've always done best when backed against a wall. At every stage of my journey I've found ways to overcome and have used those moments as fuel. I think a lot about when I was confronted by that DEA agent at the airport in San Francisco back when I was selling herb on the street. How the anxiety of it all and the threat of losing my family and ending up behind bars caused me to focus on legitimate business only. If you look back at that time, around 2010, you'll notice my music career went absolutely crazy. Between 2010 and 2013 I released more than fifteen albums and started to generate some real money in the rap game. Shortly after that I birthed CookiesSF, and the rest is history. Up against it, I'm forced to level up and figure how to change and elevate myself for the better.

The reality of being in a bad place makes you want to work nonstop and keep yourself distracted. At least that's how it's always been for me. And while that forces creativity and a drive to succeed that maybe wouldn't have existed otherwise, you make sacrifices. I sacrificed a lot, namely my peace of mind. Even when I had everything in the world—$20 million in my bank account, multiple properties, access to whatever you could dream of—my mind wouldn't allow me to enjoy it, and I kept working like I was broke. The most successful companies in my portfolio have been birthed and developed with this mindset, so maybe it's a blessing to be this dedicated to the game. But the sacrifice is real. Besides the mental exhaustion, I'm sure it can take a toll on a person's physical health as well. Hell, it just might have played a role in my colon cancer diagnosis.

. . .

As much as I was a fighter, the news that they couldn't remove the cancer broke me. Before the procedure, I was told that if they hadn't detected the polyp, I would have had six months to a year to live. Tops. That thought cycled through my head as I left the facility, escorted by a young Latina nurse I had befriended.

"Hey," she said as we made it through the exit, tears still streaming down my face, "you don't need to be crying. Right now, you need to be strong. And you need to fight." *Easy for you to say,* I thought.

"I'm serious," she said, continuing her pep talk. "You didn't know this, but I have brain cancer myself. I'm fighting right now, and you need to be fighting, too." From that moment shit got real.

Let me tell you, shit *stayed* real when the doctors x-rayed my tumor at a follow-up appointment. They determined it was late Stage 2 or early Stage 3. My surgery to remove the cancer, which had been scheduled for a month out, was moved up to just ten days out. They said they couldn't risk waiting any longer. I met so many people on my journey who were in my exact shoes. People with the same diagnosis as me, young Latino or African American men the same age as me, who are no longer here. I'm painfully aware that I am one of the lucky ones and that I had a support system around me with immediate family and close friends. Dad had retired from the restaurant business, and I moved him into my house several years earlier and he became a true caregiver, preparing most of my meals for me. My brother, Matt, was around, too, but I could tell that, like when my mother was sick, he was uncomfortable with the situation. He was distant but there if I needed him. And then there were my dogs, Buddy and Junior, who were always by my side. Man's best friend and all of that. And I also had my fans, who were constantly reaching out on social media and letting me know that I had their support, which meant the world to me.

My surgery was just ten days away, but I had booked studio time to write and record my next album, *Gotti*. It was the darkest period. I'd be spitting bars and would have to take breaks to just cry it out in the lounge or in an empty hallway. I was in the studio writing lyrics to a beat, and I didn't want everything I wrote to be like "I'm dying of cancer, remember to love me when I'm gone" type shit. Nah, fuck that. I was trying to be hard and serious, in mafia Berner mode. But meanwhile I was getting interrupted by calls from the staff at the UCSF Medical Center, where my surgery was scheduled, reading death waivers aloud to me, asking for me to acknowledge the risks of my surgery and outlining the scenario for what would happen if I didn't wake up. They were telling me, as they have to, about the multiple ways I could potentially die during my surgery or, of course, afterward. It was fucking rough.

But maybe the roughest part was the fact that the pandemic was still raging on, which meant I was going to be all alone for the operation. On the day of the surgery, my dad dropped me off at UCSF Medical Center. I walked into the brightly lit lobby by myself, traveled up the elevator, and checked in with registration. From there it all happened so fast. I was told to get undressed. I put my surgical gown on and was wheeled into an operating room that looked straight out of a sci-fi movie. My surgery was done robotically, and the OR was packed with crazy machines with wires running everywhere. I felt like I had been abducted onto an alien spacecraft and this was their lab. I remember one of the nurses asking me a question, but before I could finish answering a soft hand began rubbing my shoulders as they placed a mask around my face and, boom, I was out.

The surgery was supposed to take three hours. It ended up lasting eight and a half hours. When I finally started to come to, I could hear nurses talking about me, saying "He's on heavy meds and won't wake up anytime soon." Dazed, I grabbed my phone and immediately made a post on Instagram with a video letting my supporters know I was good, wires and tubes sticking out of me, and wrote a caption saying I'd made it through the operation. And then I passed out again. I woke up again about an hour later once the meds wore off as I was being rolled to my room. I picked up my phone to find there were more than twenty thousand comments on an Instagram post I didn't even remember posting. As you can imagine, my friends and family were extremely concerned because of how long the surgery had taken, and they were pretty upset to learn through social media that I had made it out safely. But what can I say? I don't remember posting it. Don't remember writing the caption. Don't know why I did it! I was half-awake and on a bunch of drugs. I guess it just felt natural. Over the next few days, I was tasked with regaining the ability to walk around the hospital floor on my own and to successfully poop to make sure the colon was functioning properly. After achieving both, I was released and ready to tackle my recovery. I left the hospital with a huge bandage wrapped around my stomach, super determined to bounce back and get right back to work.

. . .

By month two of recovery, I was walking short laps on my driveway and feeling strong. That's when I got another text from Doctor J: *Gilbert, can we chat?* I'd seen this movie before and instantly knew something was wrong. I called Doctor J to find out that there was still tumor DNA circulating through my bloodstream and that I needed to start an aggressive chemotherapy *yesterday*. I was crushed.

It wasn't the stomach cancer that killed my mother; it was the complications from her chemotherapy. The port they had put in her chest ended up puncturing a main vein and caused very serious blood clots. Just like that, her ten-year life expectancy turned into four months. When Doctor J said the word "chemotherapy," all I could think about was Mom. Images and moments from her final weeks and months flashed before me. Those dark days at her house. Draining the fluid from her lungs. Rubbing the ice chips on her lips when she was too weak to eat or drink. Doing anything in my power to help make her feel better, to give her any sort of relief, and feeling totally helpless the whole time.

I refused to do a port. Instead, I had to take very high doses of the chemo medicine through a PICC line in my veins. I began a brutal routine of going into UCSF every two weeks. Stinje would drive me to and from treatment, and I'll never forget one day we were sitting in the waiting room and he broke down in tears because he didn't want to see me like this anymore. I knew he wanted to be strong for me and felt so bad that he was going through this, too, so I ended up buying him a nice Rolex as a way of letting him know how much I appreciated him. Stinje has been my right-hand man since my Tully days. He's my driver, my dog sitter, my assistant—whatever is needed. He's late, he gets lost all the time and has an amazing ability to always take the wrong turn, but he's a fucking rock-solid dude who I'll ride with till the end.

Normally, the way chemotherapy treatment works is that you go in, they put the port in your chest and attach a chemo bag that drips short disbursements of medicine for a couple of weeks until you return and replace the bag. Rinse and repeat.

But because I wasn't doing the port, I would go into UCSF, lie down on a patient's table, and watch as they'd take a skinny tube and put it in a vein in my arm and run it all the way to my chest. I would get slammed with the medicine. A two-week dose in one sitting. After that was over with, I had to take the big-ass white chemo pill that any chemo survivor can tell you about. It's absolutely disgusting.

Chemo was and is by far the hardest thing I've ever been through. I couldn't breathe in the air outside and had to wrap my entire face up in a scarf like the Taliban whenever I ventured outdoors; just the act of breathing felt like I was swallowing razor blades. My toes and fingertips felt like they were constantly getting pricked by needles, and I could only manage to drink warm water. If it weren't for ginger and lemon tea, cannabis oils, and acupuncture, there was no way I could have functioned or kept any food down. I felt weak and experienced the worst nausea imaginable—anywhere I looked I felt like throwing up. It's not like I was in agonizing pain, but I sure was fucked up. I was dying.

. . .

My most vivid memory during chemo treatment is an unfortunate one. It was on my third round of treatment. I had rented a house on Stinson Beach near Mount Tamalpais State Park to get a change of scenery. Even though I couldn't really go outside, it was good for the family. I was barely hanging on and honestly felt like giving up.

But you know me—I couldn't stop working. I joined a scheduled call with the Cookies board of directors and was listening with my phone on mute as I made trips back and forth to the toilet to throw up. On this particular day, my body felt the worst it ever had. The chemo had beaten me down pretty bad. The worst was still to come.

At the time, the board consisted of Jai, who despite our turbulence over the years had remained a partner, Parker, myself, and a representative for the billionaire and SI, our biggest investor. The purpose of the board is to oversee the business; it's where all the major decisions in the company are made. Each member gets an equal vote. The most important traits that I think a board member can have are passion, honesty, loyalty, and dedication.

On the call, the representative dropped the bombshell: SI had decided to stop funding us further, because he no longer believed our company still held value. It was a shocking assessment, considering it was founded on pure bullshit.

I took myself off mute.

"You know, for the last couple hours while you've been talking, I've been throwing up and in the worst shape of my life. You know I'm sick," I said, clearly hurt, "but not one of you have taken a moment to ask if I was even feeling OK."

"I'm not your friend," the representative responded coldly. "I'm your investor."

Never mind that it was the most inhumane shit I'd ever heard, but this became the exact moment I realized that I was fighting for my life and my company at the same time.

I should have seen the signs right away. From the jump, they wanted us to raise more than $100 million, which would have diluted my stake down way too much because our valuation simply wasn't there yet. Instead, Parker and I came up with the asset-light model, which allowed us to expand without needing to raise a ton of capital. As Cookies executives, Parker and I have an obligation to do what is best for the company and its shareholders—not necessarily what is best for a single one of its lenders, which SI was at the time.

In the months leading up to the board call, SI had been pushing for more control of the company. They were working toward buying out Jai's equity for $70+ million, wanted as much equity as they could from me, and wanted to buy CookiesSF for over $150 million.

Shortly before the board call, they backed down from all of it. Instead of buying CookiesSF, they literally just ghosted me. Blue texts sent. Nothing read. No responses. That was when I first realized something weird was going on, to say the least. The confirmation came during that board call. Now they were requesting a change in leadership, which was ultimately a play to take control of the board. Whoever controls the board pretty much controls the company.

On the call, they shocked us by saying we were uninvestable and that they had made a mistake putting money into our company and weren't going to fund us further. We were stunned. Why the sudden change?

When SI initially invested the $10 million in 2019, they confidently told us, "That's not enough, you'll go through that in a year." I think they were surprised that we were expanding so fast without the capital. That wasn't what they wanted. I also think that—and I am trying to be respectful even though they are, aside from cancer, the worst thing that has ever happened to me—they had good intentions in the beginning. But they'd made mistakes investing in other businesses and we were one of the companies where they had a shot at getting their money back, or a sizable return on their investment. Cookies is a real brand with real motion and a ton of value behind it. I think they just decided, "Fuck it, let's take the whole pie."

They informed me that they would stop the incoming funds unless I got rid of Parker. They were trying to superfuck the guy. I was warned that if I didn't get rid of Parker, I would be dealing with hell. But if I did remove him and bring in new leadership, then they would give me a hall pass. That was never an option. Not for a second. Parker knew my business head to toe, was fully invested in it, and worked harder for it than anyone I know. Besides, he is the only reason I'm still alive, and you can't break that kind of bond. Also, if they had gotten rid of Parker, I'm convinced they would have brought in some former Nike or Coca-Cola executive who would have raised hundreds of millions of dollars, diluted me down to nothing, gained control over the board, used me until it was time for an exit, and then removed me for cause and—maybe—given me a baby piece for participation. That's how these guys operate.

The board seat represented by SI seemed to try blocking every move the business made to survive and grow. I was living a nightmare. Imagine being in your prime as a businessperson, feeling the juice I felt with the rise of Cookies. Then, you're hit with cancer, undergoing terrible chemo treatments, having to deal with not only the fear of dying but also the possibility of losing the only security you have for your children. The comfort I took in leaving a legacy behind was being pulled right out from under me.

I did one more round of chemo and decided I couldn't take any more. I decided to tap out and accept whatever the universe had in store for me.

. . .

I was weak with nerve damage from my illness, and the doctors told me it would be months still until I was back on my feet and feeling anything close to normal again. But 4/20 was around the corner, and for the first time ever Golden Gate Park was hosting performances on the legendary Hippie Hill. Thirty thousand people were set to attend, and I knew that to rock a stage in my hometown, to feel the love and energy from my people, would be the best medicine in the world.

When April 20 rolled around, I wasn't anywhere near even 50 percent healthy, but I arrived at Golden Gate Park feeling on top of the world. When I jumped on the stage, the sea of people screamed and huge clouds of smoke began emerging from the crowd. I had goosebumps during the entire performance. Not only had it been a life goal to be on that stage, but the moment was exhilarating—and a much-needed reminder of who the fuck I was.

Dark clouds were still forming with the SI group, but we continued to pump life into the business. Parker and I were finding new channels to bring in capital in a non-dilutive way, and a crazy wave of motion for the brand kicked off when the mainstream media started paying attention to our growth and what we were doing.

In the summer of 2021, I returned to my beautiful estate in Montana for the first time since my cancer diagnosis a year earlier and barely got settled in before receiving a call from Kim Baron, my head of PR. She told me that *Forbes* magazine was interested in doing an interview with me and was even considering featuring me on the cover. Kim asked if I could fly out to New York for the interview. I stared out at the lake and mountain view from my dock, one of the few times I've ever been speechless.

I regained my composure and asked if the cover was a sure thing.

Kim said that they couldn't confirm it at that moment and wouldn't likely know until closer to the publishing date. I looked back out at the lake, saw my daughter swimming, glanced toward my boat, and made one of the hardest decisions of my career. "I know it's an honor and one of the greatest opportunities in business and a major compliment to our brand," I said. "But I really just want to soak up this moment with my family," I told her. "Traveling to New York right now just isn't in the cards."

When I was in that hospital bed recovering from my surgery, I dreamt of a moment just like this one, being with my family in Montana, enjoying the calm and beauty of the lake life. I spent the next several hours daydreaming of what being on the cover of *Forbes* would be like, but I was content with my decision. That night, I threw some jerk chicken that I'd been marinating all day onto the grill.

That's when Kim called me back and asked, "What if the writer flew to you for the interview?"

I told her, then I'd be happy to do it. She confirmed that the writer was up for the trip and would be there in two days and that a photographer would come by the day after for the potential cover shoot. There was only one problem: I had no outfit to wear, and there wasn't exactly a place to shop for such a monumental moment here in my spot in the middle of nowhere Montana. So I called up Stinje, asked him to grab from my crib a new leather jacket with a stunning gray fur collar I had just purchased, and put him on a plane to Montana, jacket in hand. It wasn't until the photo shoot was about to begin that I realized I didn't have any jeans or shoes to match the outfit. So we shot it from the waist up while I wore basketball shorts. The photo of me that made it onto the *Forbes* cover, wearing that fly jacket and staring into the camera with all the confidence in the world, was the very first test shot we took. After the test shots, the photographer suggested I smoke before we took the real shots, but once the shoot began I think he realized it wasn't the best call; my eyes were *way* too low to be on the cover of *Forbes* fuckin' magazine.

That cover changed my life and helped make me and Cookies as relevant as ever. Soon after, *Rolling Stone* magazine released a list of the richest rappers on the planet. The top five, in order, read: Jay-Z, Diddy, Kanye, me, and Dr. Dre . . . All of this while being starved out by hostile investors who were telling me my company was worthless.

We carried that momentum, opening our Las Vegas store right on the strip. During the grand opening, customers lined up around the block. Many of them discovered a tattoo shop across the street and, while they waited, about fifty people got the Cookies logo tattooed on their bodies. Today, that store is a *destination* whenever you hit the strip.

In October 2022, right before my thirty-ninth birthday, we opened our New York City store, a five-floor mega complex in Herald Square on West 34th Street across from the iconic Macy's department store. Once again, the line of fans and customers was long—multiple city blocks—and the crowd was in a frenzy. They had to shut down the street, and it felt like complete pandemonium. Because the sale of recreational cannabis hadn't been passed yet in New York, the opening was only for CookiesSF clothing but with the intention of becoming a dispensary as soon as the city allowed it, which happened a year later, in 2023. Hundreds, if not thousands, of people were celebrating the Cookies brand coming to New York City, and the party was taking place right there in the middle of the street. Epic.

. . .

Then, just a few days before Christmas, the investors at SI filed a lawsuit against us. Parker and I were back in New York, in town on business to raise some capital—which SI had already stopped doing at that point. We were in the lounge at our Herald Square location, vibing out, smoking weed, and enjoying the energy with friends and staff. Parker's phone buzzed, and I saw him look at his screen. My boy literally turned white as a ghost. I asked what was going on—I thought I saw him stop breathing for a second. I'd never seen him like that before.

Over the next year they hit us hard in what I can only describe as a coordinated attack, and the lawsuits began. In one case, Cookies was sued for more than $100 million by a group of SI-backed investors called Cookies Retail, LLC (CRE) on claims of misrepresentation and other wild accusations.

SI was working with CRE to build an alter ego company to CRE called TRP, raising money on the Cookies IP on the claim that they had licensing rights with us (not true), saying that they had production rights to Cookies around the world (not true), and laying claim to our retail portfolio. The last text the billionaire investor sent me was a note telling me that I had better hire a lawyer who knew what they were doing. I must say, I'm glad I listened. These guys were plotting big-time, trying to raise money under the brand's IP, and then trying to wash us. It was clear that their strategy was to starve us out, which is wild, 'cause that's the same way you kill cancer.

The lawsuit revealed a targeted attack against us. There were even texts referencing a "Blue Wedding"—like the Red Wedding in *Game of Thrones,* where a family is brought together under the guise of unity and then ambushed and hacked to death.

This wasn't simply a business dispute. They were lying on our names and making outrageously false claims that included fraud, theft, and corruption. It kept coming like a train crash. First, they filed in public court, but the case was actually required to go to arbitration, which is private. So while the case was a public matter they could and did issue statements that smeared us, but once we were in arbitration we couldn't respond publicly. Without a voice to the public, we just had to take it on the chin.

No matter how hot the brand was, the business was hurting. CRE controlled thirty of our seventy stores. Once the lawsuit was filed, they just stopped paying royalties. And they owed us $8 million in royalties. If we had been getting that, we wouldn't have had any problems. Instead, we were hamstrung. We couldn't make payroll, we couldn't do all the marketing we had planned. CRE had squatting rights—the right to open up stores—in Pennsylvania, Ohio, and a couple other markets, but they didn't, so we felt we couldn't expand like we wanted to. It put us in a hole.

After an exhausting legal battle, in 2025 an arbitrator sided with Cookies fully. CRE got nothing and Cookies was awarded more than $23 million. I felt vindicated, sure, but there had been a painful lesson. I learned that the true hindrance of being litigated on is that nobody—and I mean nobody—wants to fuck with you.

. . .

SI had a representative on the board, and they were able to block any opportunity for growth or investment thanks to the predatory covenants that were part of their note. When someone invests in you at an early stage, there are often provisions placed like this for some protection for minority equity holders. It's like, "I'll invest with you, but you can't do X or Y without our permission." The only way for us to retire those covenants was through a qualified round of financing above $10 million, which was almost impossible to raise at that time—because nobody invests into a company while it's in litigation.

With these controlling notes, they were able to literally freeze our business. We couldn't get production funds, we couldn't get capital raised, we couldn't do anything. It was just "no," "no," "no." This stopped any strategic investments we were working on, and the smear campaigns were damaging our public image not long after I'd gotten me and the brand on the damn cover of *Forbes*. They had endless money and had made it very clear they wouldn't stop until we were starved out.

And that's when the universe played its hand.

When an investor invests through a note, there is a maturity date. With respect to the notes we issued, including to SI, when the maturity date approached, the notes would either come due, or investors could elect to extend their note or convert it into equity. Under the notes, investors had to notify the company of their decision of whether they wanted to extend or convert into equity at least ten days before the maturity date. If an investor didn't timely notify the company, its note would become due and they would become an unsecured creditor with the right to get back their investment along with 2.55 percent interest. It's meant to dissuade investors from missing the window and ghosting their lenders. I mean, who the hell is loaning $10 million for a 2.55 percent return?

Ten days before the maturity date we began to hear from a couple of our investors who had been elected to extend the maturity date of their notes. No word from SI. They could extend and keep our nightmare going. Or they could convert into millions in equity in the company. But if the window passed and we didn't hear from

SI, of course, it meant we could pay them their $10 million plus interest and walk away.

On the eve before the tenth and final day there was still no word from SI. I couldn't take my eyes off the clock in my kitchen, where Parker and I were awaiting our fate. "No way, bro. No way," Parker kept saying. "No way they're going to miss this. Investors of this caliber? There's no way seasoned institutional investors would ever miss something like this."

I felt differently. They weren't even paying attention to the game like that, I thought. They're too busy suing us and had a lot of other businesses to distract them. They were invested in other things and weren't taking their job as seriously as we take ours. They didn't eat, live, breathe, and piss this like we did.

That night, I spoke to the moon.

I walked out onto my balcony and lit a nicely rolled joint. The stars were shining wild, and there was a full moon in the sky. I closed my eyes and could feel the brightness hit my face. I breathed in hella deep. In through my nose. *Smell the flower*. Out through my mouth. *Blow out the candle*. For three minutes, I kept going like this as I got into a kind of trance. *Yo, we are going to win this,* I said over and over in my imaginary dialogue with the moon. *They're going to miss this date*. For three minutes I stood there with my eyes closed, letting the joint burn between my fingers, and I manifested it.

The next day, I met up with Parker at the Cookies compound and told him that we had nothing to worry about, they were going to miss the date to extend or convert their note. He wouldn't entertain it for a second. All day we waited for an email, a text, anything from SI. We checked the physical mail, had all employees check their emails, and even opened up our P.O. box. By the end of the day, the maturity date had officially passed. Sure enough, they had missed it. That meant that SI was now an unsecured creditor, and we had the right to pay off their note and be rid of all its restrictive provisions.

We sent them a letter saying, "We'll pay you your $10 million back plus the interest. Here's your $11 million."

We weren't out of litigation hell completely. But we are still here. It was like our business was reborn. And it comes down to everything I've talked about in this book. By being laser-focused on our business, being hands-on and aware and involved in every part of it, we were on top of our shit.

They dropped the ball.

When your back is against the wall, you'll be forced to find ways to survive. I'm willing to bet that Bill Gates, Jeff Bezos, Elon Musk, all those big boys have faced similar moments as entrepreneurs. Being a creative ninja when it's time to get something done is what it takes to be a billionaire. Straight up. Some people feel like no matter what, they'll figure it out. On the flip side, others give up too easily. Others in my shoes would have given Parker up, no questions asked.

. . .

I've been the underdog my whole career. I've overcome hostile legal and business situations by being honest and staying on top of my business. And I did it while staring down the barrel of death.

Like I've said, I do my best work with my back against the wall. As I sit here in my boardroom, I'm staring at a screenshot I had printed out, framed, and hung on the wall. It's a tweet from *Billboard* from December 2021, right around the time the SI lawsuit dropped. It reads:

This week's top-selling albums:

1. Adele, *30*
2. Taylor Swift, *Red*
3. Berner, *Gotti*
4. Olivia Rodrigo, *Sour*
5. The Beatles, *Let It Be* soundtrack

When I thought I was going to die, I recorded my bestselling album yet. You'd be surprised what you're capable of. When you're under pressure, you'll find ways that you never imagined to get things done. It's why I'm so proud of what we've achieved in the last few years with limited capital and in the face of multiple lawsuits. When those with wicked motives came after me, the universe let the good prevail. The whole journey has been an emotional roller coaster, but I wouldn't change it for the world. **You have to be down to come up, and it's the struggles that make the successes so enjoyable.** That's the story of my whole career. In this game, to constantly fight for what you have is what separates the men from the boys. The whales from the sharks. My goal was always to build a brand and company so strong that nobody could tear it apart. For the first time in three years, I believe that I've achieved that. Pressure makes diamonds, and Cookies is a flawless stone.

420
Hippie Hill
20
20

Chapter 11

PUT YOUR FINGERPRINTS ON *EVERYTHING*

In my experience, the middleman always has an agenda—and chances are, it may not be the same as yours. Managers, agents, negotiators, mediators . . . their motivations can seriously hurt—or even kill—a lot of promising deals. I've seen it happen time and again. It's why I try to eliminate the middleman whenever I can.

Being hands-on has gotten me where I am today. From representing myself in negotiations to designing Cookies stores, overseeing quality control of our products, and handling all my social media channels, it's the only way I can make sure my business is an authentic representation of myself. It's one thing to share an idea. It's a whole other animal to be able to clearly lay out your vision from the heart with investors and business partners and work together to achieve it.

I'm the CEO of my record label, my rolling paper company, my clothing company, and the Cookies cannabis empire. No matter the venture, I make sure I stay on top of it all and talk directly to my leadership and creative teams as much as I can. That approach is crucial when you are the visionary. If you are a hands-on founder, you will gain respect from your teams, who will in turn be more motivated to help your business grow. More importantly, seeing your vision through from start to finish will keep you from having to constantly put out fires.

Not a day goes by that I'm not reminded of why I put my fingerprints on everything I do. As I write this, I'm in the skies on a flight from Spain to the Netherlands, where I'm hosting a release party in Amsterdam for my album, Hoffa. *I thought of the idea of plastering the whole city with my album art to build up the buzz. I had the same idea when we were in Spain, and left it to the label to handle. It never got done. The posters never made it out of the box. So guess who is personally sending art files to printers and meeting with the team on the ground in Amsterdam to execute the campaign? That's right: me.*

I've taught myself how to take a dream and turn it into a reality. During each step of that process, I've learned that if you want to make things happen, sometimes you just have to do it yourself.

. . .

Some nights, long after my team has gone home, I find myself walking around the twenty-thousand-square-foot Cookies compound all alone. Into the beautiful, functional, custom-built kitchen with state-of-the-art cooktops and floor-to-ceiling custom tiles. Across the boardroom with the Italian-made leather chairs and enormous oak conference table with the *Cookies* logo in neon lights hanging from the ceiling above, so massive that each letter is the size of a grown-ass man. Walking around here feels like I'm living in a dream that I don't want to wake up from, like I can't fucking believe this is real life. I walk past the plaques and photo murals from store openings hanging on the painted blue walls, beyond the incredible art pieces, and around the show-stopping original Dustin Yellin sculpture in the middle of the main lounge.

I'll spark one up, kick back in one of the lounges—every surface illuminated in Cookies blue—and ask myself if I could have better spent or invested the $9 million it took to buy and build this creative space. Any way I slice it, the answer is always the same: no.

The compound has only been around for a couple of years now, but it's already proven to be the perfect setup for growing my businesses. Here I can be at my best as a leader and entrepreneur: hands-on.

The building was originally an old warehouse. I got the inspiration to construct it after visiting Snoop Dogg's place a few years back, which felt like a clubhouse for him and his crew. There was a full-size basketball court and all sorts of fun shit, including a studio, a green screen, and multiple media rooms. As I left, I remember thinking, *This is pretty cool. There's something going on here.* In my head, I began mapping out how my own compound would look and feel. But what I saw that day was mostly a lot of hanging out. That's fine and all, but I knew that if I was going to create my own version, I needed a space that would inspire creativity and productivity.

The entire upstairs is built for media production. There are podcast studios, music studios, tools for graphic designers, a large green screen, and a suite of video editing bays. (In 2023 I co-wrote and produced a feature-length film, *Splash City,* and I'm proud to say all the postproduction was done in-house.) The walls are adorned with art, and from the moment you step into the space, you can feel that it's an environment that fosters imagination and inspiration. It's a place designed for you to create, including cozy furniture and all the amenities you could want. After all, to be creative you have to be comfortable.

Downstairs is a main lounge connected to one of the several boardrooms and a mock dispensary where all our product and merchandise is displayed, just as it would be in one of the Cookies retail shops. I love inviting business associates to the compound and working out deals here. When I designed it, I put myself in their shoes and had the whole experience mapped out in my head. Now, it's my reality: I can entertain and host, with a private chef cooking for us while we discuss business. Then, we eat a choice meal in a vibey room before heading into a private boardroom to continue discussions. Believe me, from the moment you walk through the door, it's hard to say "no" to closing a deal. And that's by design.

You have to understand: We never had an office like this before. I never had an office, *period.* What was I going to do with a traditional office? I never wanted that. I built Cookies in the front room of my house—and not just in the start-up days. When the company was generating hundreds of millions in revenue, I was holding design sessions with the homies on my team in my kitchen and meeting with cannabis breeders on park benches, setting up multimillion-dollar deals in a grocery store parking lot and closing them in the back of my Escalade. I didn't have a dedicated office space and didn't trust people I didn't know coming by my house. You don't bring people where you sleep.

I never wanted a typical office, but the compound is different. It's a representation of me, my business, and the values that are important to our growth. I waited until a time when we could do it right, and I'm glad I did. Now that we have it, the kind of deals we're closing there are insane. I'm sure most people tour the place and assume it's just a great spot to chill and smoke herb and do business. Don't get me wrong—it is. But when I look around, what I see is totally different: I see a space that allows me to touch every part of my business all at once.

I can meet with my designers, my marketing team, the film department, breeders, sales and finance teams, musical artists, producers, retail partners, cultivation partners, you name it—all in one building. I can jump into any conversation or creative session and see what's happening and provide input in real time. **A powerful CEO who is a true visionary has to touch everything.**

. . .

The compound was built to feed my true addiction, which is being hands-on. I'm not sure exactly where this addiction came from. But I'm trying to think of a time when I approached things differently, and to be real, I'm coming up empty. I think being so hands-on stems from being passionate about what I do, while also believing in the old saying that if you want something done right you have to do it yourself.

Growing up, I saw how good my mom was at working with people, and I credit her for a lot of the communication skills I've learned. But I remember watching how involved my dad was with his restaurant business, and there's no doubt that rubbed off on me, too. A passionate chef is *definitely* going to stay on top of everything going on in their kitchen.

So I've never been afraid to get my hands dirty. And it's worked for me. Sometimes I think it's the *doing* that I'm actually addicted to. I remember in the early days of my music career, which was essentially the first legal business I built with my label, Bern One Entertainment, I would head down to the facility that prints the

CD labels and posters and meticulously look at the mock-ups and watch it all get printed. I quickly realized that it's important to have a relationship with the person doing the job. Because I was there in-person working with the printer, I didn't have to call up like everyone else and say, *"Hi, my name is Gilbert Milam, and I placed an order on Monday . . ."* Instead, I had a direct line to the manufacturer. So it was more like *"Hey, Frank, it's Berner. I came in on Monday and paid for these posters. You said they'd be ready in two days. What's going on?"* All those years of schooling have their place, and if you have an MBA, a JD, or a PhD, all the power to you. But I learned by DIY. It's the only way I know. Everything I know I picked up by getting my hands dirty; I firmly believe it's what keeps me in the game. **Being hands-on will allow you to form a deeper connection with the people that can help enable your business to grow.**

Don't get it twisted. You'll need to surround yourself with a dedicated team you trust, and you will have to learn to delegate. But if you aren't actively involved in every aspect of your company—if your fingerprints aren't on literally every part of your business—the results could be catastrophic. I truly believe that the entire fate of many companies hangs, by a thread, on department heads that have zero direct communication with a CEO or founder. Inevitably, stuff gets lost in communication. It's why I listen to every mix and give detailed feedback on the records I'm making. It's why I help direct and edit my own music videos and provide direction to designers for the clothing and to packagers for the herb products. It's why I consult with our breeders as we develop new cannabis menus and provide my own tasting notes. It's why I speak directly with investors about the current state of the business and where we want to go and listen in on marketing calls for all my companies to ensure that we come across authentic and that everybody is being heard. As a CEO, having a direct line open with all aspects of your business not only gets situations figured out faster but it keeps your vision crystal clear.

Having a buffer is necessary at times, especially when it comes to the areas of your business that require a specific expertise, like a tax accountant or financial manager. But even then, it's to your benefit to stay involved. I learned that one the hard way.

About a decade ago when Cookies was getting off the ground and the revenue started rolling in, I hired a business management firm to handle all my financial affairs. It was run by someone we'll call "Russ." From the jump I gave Russ 5 percent of my income, and in exchange I let him take care of everything—paying bills, taxes, all of it. I thought that's what rich dudes do. As I started to accumulate some *real* money through my various revenue streams, I'd hit up Russ on the phone or via text with questions.

"How we looking on taxes?" I'd ask. "Are we putting money aside for taxes?"

I'm an anxious dude to begin with, and I'd heard horror stories of entrepreneurs who didn't understand how taxes work and never budgeted for it and nearly went broke as a result.

"You're the man, Berner. Don't worry about it," he'd reply to my countless inquiries. "You're the boss. Just let me take care of all of that."

I'm not interested in surrounding myself with yes-men, and something felt off right away. After a bunch of conversations like that one, I ended up getting frustrated with Russ and switched firms. Soon after, I got a call from my new firm.

"You know you have a bunch of unpaid taxes, right?"

You've got to be fucking kidding me, I thought.

"No," was all I could spit out.

When we looked into it, it turned out that Russ had never filed taxes. Nothing. He hadn't even prepared them. There were forms where he was supposed to fill in certain information like my business number. I looked at one of the forms and the business number just read "12345678." I couldn't believe it. I sued him and his firm. They ended up covering the penalties from the unpaid taxes, but the experience changed the way I handle my shit.

Now, I talk to my business manager on the phone every single day to develop that trust and that relationship, which helps me navigate it all. I look at my bank statements. I study my annual reports. I read through all the deals we make and discuss all the elements with my biz guy. I make sure to be *very* hands-on. I know plenty of rappers and entertainers and people with money who would never talk to their financial guy and would just trust that things are being handled.

. . .

I can't tell you how many times being hands-on has saved my ass. Especially in a nontraditional industry like cannabis, where practices entrepreneurs may take for granted—the willingness of banks to accept your money, or the option of writing off business expenses—are not a given.

I make sure I'm hands-on in every avenue. Just recently I had a sample clearance issue with one of my songs. The owner of the estate denied my clearance request because of vulgar lyrics in my record. Normally in this situation, an artist would have their attorney go back and forth with the estate until a settlement could be reached. But you know me. I chose to write an email from the heart directly to the artist's estate. I explained my situation—who I was, where I was coming from lyrically, and my intentions with this track. The estate appreciated it so much. They even told me that no artist had ever reached out personally like I had and explained their lyrics. Ultimately, they ended up clearing the sample.

Even more recently, a partnership with one of our cultivators started to get a little rocky. They wanted more money for a strain they were growing (using our genetics, by the way) and didn't want to offer us the product anymore, even though it was rightfully ours to package and sell. The product had a ton of hype, and I could tell they wanted to capitalize on that hype and start building their own brand. This was an important partner for us, so with the relationship on the brink of deteriorating, I jumped on a call with the cultivator to sort out a solution. My approach was simple: I offered to help them create a brand, name, and logo, and to put that logo on the products they grew for us and gave them permission to grow a few of our proprietary genetics under their brand name. I even got them shelf space in our stores. Problem solved.

Had I left this in the hands of my business development team, as most CEOs would have done, we likely would have had to abandon the partnership. My being hands-on changed all that, and I really believe that hearing from me directly made a difference to that partner.

I always want to make myself available, and I think it helps to see a CEO who is so personally involved in their work. I'm regularly called into investor meetings as a way to bring up the morale in the room. Hell, I can remember plenty of times already at the compound where I've personally cooked fire-ass meals during a capital raise to help make things feel special and unique. Bringing investors into my space and cooking them something from the soul opens up conversations in a whole new way. It's unique. It's authentic. It's personal. Most importantly, it separates us from others.

. . .

Put your fingerprints on the deals you make, too. Representing yourself in negotiations can be an extremely powerful approach. The way I see it, nobody is more motivated to see a deal through than yourself.

I've got a gift. I can sell ice to an Eskimo. Put me in a room and I know how to get people excited, interested, and committed to an idea—and I'm straight-up while doing it. So you can imagine how hard I've found it to watch an agent or manager pitch or negotiate on my behalf. When I first started gaining traction in the music industry, I hired an agency who would work to land me live gigs. They'd bring me offers to play sets for $5K and expect me to jump and settle for it. About five years ago, underwhelmed, I decided to part ways with them and took full rein of my own bookings. Pretty soon after, I started negotiating paychecks for twenty, thirty, and eventually up to sixty thousand for a show. Sometimes more . . . a lot more. In 2022, the Smokers Club festival in Southern California was about to go down. They had a huge lineup set with major artists locked in, including A$AP Rocky, Kid Cudi, and Playboi Carti. It being a big weed-themed festival, they reached out to me to be a part of the event. Back in the day, a festival gig like this was a $10,000 payday for me. After sitting down at the negotiation table myself with the festival organizers, I was able to explain the authenticity I would bring to the event and locked in $250,000 for a twenty-minute set. To this day it's the highest-paying gig I've ever done.

I'll give you one more example: In the summer of 2023, some reps from William Morris called me and asked if I would join Snoop and Wiz Khalifa on their tour. I told them that I planned on enjoying my lake house for the summer and wouldn't be able to justify going on tour during those two months unless I was making fifty to sixty thousand each night. We eventually settled on $40,000 per night, and I ended up earning $1.4 million just from the shows on that tour. I honestly don't think that would have happened if it were my agent on the other end of the call instead. Who can advocate for me better than me?

The way I see it, letting someone else represent you leaves a lot of room for error and a ton of shit out of your control. You have to remember how easily deals can fall apart. If someone is negotiating for you, they can kill a deal in a matter of minutes just based on how they speak or carry themselves or what their body language is. If you're as passionate about your business as I am about mine, then it basically feels like you're putting your entire life in another person's hands. And most of the time, that person likely has ulterior motives you might not even be aware of, like commissions or other hidden agendas.

I've seen so many deals fall apart because of the man in the middle. I remember being in the studio with superstar Puerto Rican singer Ozuna to record an album together. The album was supposed to be part of a bigger brand partnership that was going to include a documentary and a new Cookies dispensary store in Puerto Rico.

When the session wrapped, Ozuna and I stepped out of the recording booth, and five people—all representing Ozuna—sat us down and started discussing business. The whole time, Ozuna sat quietly among us and didn't say a word. It was the weirdest thing ever. These dudes spoke as if he wasn't even there. They were extremely aggressive in their pitches and came off super arrogant. It was a total turnoff. The more they spoke, the more I thought, *Why doesn't Ozuna jump in and save this conversation? Or at least just speak for himself?* The deal had so much potential, but it fell apart then and there. As I left the studio, I was down that we couldn't make something work, but in that moment I found comfort knowing that would never happen to me.

That wasn't anywhere near the biggest deal I ever saw a middleman fuck up. In the early 2000s, I sent an email to an artist—I won't say the artist's name, but it is someone super influential in the cannabis space. Not only someone I had worked with but who I considered a friend. I pitched a marijuana lifestyle brand that included clothing, merchandise, and tons of accessories like rolling trays, papers, stackable jars, and smell-proof bags. Out of courtesy, I cc'd the artist's manager to keep them in the loop.

A few days later, I got a phone call from the manager. He was irate. He told me I had crossed a boundary by sending that email and reaching out directly to the artist and to never step over the line like that. He killed the deal right then and there. That business idea, if you haven't figured it out, turned into the Cookies SF empire. A billion-dollar business. Damn shame.

All these years later, that exchange with that manager is one of the reasons I choose to have important conversations myself and not through a mediator. If you're selling something, you have to know the product. You have to know what makes it great, how it's made, who is buying it, and how to reach them. And you need to be able to communicate that vision yourself.

. . .

To articulate your vision is one thing. To get people to listen is a whole other beast. When I was coming up, to find an audience you needed either a mic in your hand or TV exposure. I'm talking one-in-a-million opportunities, like an album breaking through or making the cast of *The Real World*. But these days? It's never been easier to find an audience. Building and maintaining one, on the other hand . . . that takes some work.

I saw the potential for social media early and knew for a fact it was a crazy-effective way to reach people. From the time I first entered the Hemp Center as a wide-eyed kid to building my multimillion-dollar compound and growing Cookies into an iconic international brand, I've had a camera in my hand to document every step along the way, and I've shared it online religiously.

I've been the person running the social media pages for myself and my companies from the very beginning. I told you I had an addiction to being hands-on. Sure, it's tedious work. My fingers are burning by the end of the day from typing on my phone, but I'm deeply connected to my social channels and see every comment that comes through—good, bad, and ugly. It's so important to talk to your customers and engage with them, especially as the founder of a company. Trust me, if you show up authentically, your customers will appreciate it and love you for it. Before you know it, you'll have built a genuine cult following.

I've always wanted to be seen. When I was eighteen years old, I auditioned for MTV's *The Real World,* the OG reality show. I put together an audition tape and sent it to the producers, hoping to hell that I would be put in the cast. I figured that if I could be seen by a national TV audience, then I would become known to people. And that would open doors for me.

I didn't get cast, and my *Real World* plan turned out to be a far reach. But over time new platforms were created that would help me accomplish the same thing and reach an even larger audience. I'm talking *worldwide.*

The combination of documenting my journey, putting it in front of people via social media, and then building a brand with those same people as my core customer base has worked wonders. I looked at social media as an incredible tool. I still do, and it's become a natural extension of my authentic self. My fans know that I'm not farming my social media out to some third-party publicity firm like so many other celebrities do. Think about it: How you engage with fans and customers will determine how you are perceived in the world.

I'll never forget the day I learned that lesson.

I've always hated sports, but growing up in San Francisco in the '80s and '90s, you couldn't escape the San Francisco 49ers football team. They were winning Super Bowls and were crazy popular in the Bay Area. Joe Montana, the superstar quarterback, might have been the most famous person in SF in those days. One late summer day, my dad took me to watch the Niners training camp. The crowd wasn't very big, and as practice wrapped for the day we were all able to head down to the field and stand near the sidelines as the players made their way off the field and into the locker room. I was standing in the sun, wiping the sweat off my forehead and waiting until Dad would tell me we could finally go home, when out of the corner of my eye I saw Joe Montana approaching. As he got near, I held out a pen and paper and asked him for his autograph. He never broke his stride. Didn't say a word, just kept walking right by me. Didn't so much as look at me, as if I didn't exist. Fine. That's his choice.

A few seconds later, the team's other quarterback, Steve Young, walked by. This was 1990, and Young was Montana's backup. I must have looked sad or something, because Young came right up to me. "Hey, kid. I'm sorry he did that," he said. "Let me give you my autograph." I wasn't a football fan and genuinely didn't know who Steve Young was. But I vividly remember leaving that practice thinking, *I really like that Steve guy*. Within a few years, Young took over from Montana and became a huge star. And I was the biggest Steve Young fan in the world, even though I still fuckin' hated sports.

That moment stayed with me. I always thought, "If I'm ever lucky enough to have fans, *that's* how I want them to think of me. That's how I want to behave."

If someone hits me up and says they listen to my music, I don't think twice about replying to say, "Thank you, I really appreciate that—and keep an eye out because I'm working on this or that and I think you'll like that, too." Chances are they'll tell their friends, "Hey, I talked to Berner, and that guy is cool. He's a real one." That shit spreads. You can be a dick, and that reputation will spread. Or you can be cool and genuine, and that will spread, too.

Whether it's responding to an angry customer, following fans who purchased your album, thanking someone for showing love, wishing a stranger a Merry Christmas, or just hitting "like" on a fan's comment, those seemingly small actions are the key to building a core audience. People used to give me a hard time for being so hands-on with my community. I remember being made fun of for filming videos of myself fulfilling orders in my living room. I'd hear snickers as I set up a camera to film myself rapping in the studio, and my boys would tease me for getting into it with trolls on the Bay Area Rap Talk message boards. But you know what? That's how people knew I was 100 percent dedicated and personally involved in everything I was building.

Too many celebrities post pointless pictures of themselves on their socials. They're missing a golden opportunity. I use those platforms to build relationships with my supporters and customers. People want to be able to touch you. They want to share a special moment with you and share their love for your product. But more than anything they want to feel that you are relatable and a real human being. I have a core audience, and I swear it's like we all grew up together. The internet and social media—and the way I approach it—have been central to that. Get to know your customers. Engage and build with them and let them know you as a person and not as a brand. I promise it will pay off in the long run.

. . .

They say the best way to learn is by doing it yourself. It's the truth. I've been able to learn all the corners of my business by taking a hands-on approach. And it might just be the best argument for being a hands-on entrepreneur.

I never graduated high school. I damn sure never went to college. And yet here I am, being invited to speak at places like the Harvard Business School to give students advice on marketing, branding, and growing a business. None of it would be possible if I hadn't built my own businesses from the ground up, with the life lessons and experiences gained along the way to the top. I tell people all the time: If you want to be successful, try putting your own money behind yourself, and then *go for it*. There's something about the risk of losing your own money that will make you focus and get your hands dirty.

I know I'm addicted to work. I'm even more hooked on being closely involved in everything I touch. If I was any other way, I wouldn't have been on the cover of *Forbes* magazine or been featured in *The New York Times*. I would have never won a Clio Award or been the first cannabis brand to win *Ad Age*'s prestigious Brand of the Year award. If I wasn't so hands-on and passionate in building my business, I would never be where I am today.

100
years

Chapter 12

A HUNDRED-YEAR BRAND

If you ever get a second shot at life, make sure you understand how blessed you truly are. For me, the second shot at life is feeling a lot more peaceful than the first. I grew up nervous and carried fears with me, like flying. Or dying young. At thirty-eight I beat colon cancer, and facing death like that has completely changed my outlook on life. Things that bothered me and weighed heavy on my chest don't seem to affect me as much anymore. Business conflicts, people's negative energy and opinions, I deal with it all differently now. I'm even overcoming my fear of flying.

I've never felt more optimistic for my future, and that's because I am still here. I'll be able to be there for my three kids. To see my eighteen-year-old daughter graduate and to watch my one-year-old son grow up. I'll be there to welcome my new baby girl into this world. There was a time when none of that seemed possible. At one point early on during my chemo treatment, I had to freeze my sperm, because I was told it was the only chance if I ever wanted to have kids again. Well, they can keep that shit in the freezer because, sure enough, my two children with my fiancée Ashley were both conceived after my diagnosis . . . 100 percent naturally. It's a great feeling to not have to be so worried all the time and to be able to value things I took for granted before. Pushing my baby's stroller around the block, cooking dinner for the family on the grill, or going to the farmers market on Sundays has never felt so good.

The world is in a weird place, and so is my business. But I'm still here, alive to fight the good fight. I'm grateful to be looking at life through a whole new lens.

. . .

I walked away from chemo treatment in 2022. I backed out. I was done with it. I knew I was taking a chance, but so far I've been lucky, and I'm in remission. I still have to go back to UCSF, where I have nothing but mad love and appreciation for the doctors and nurses who took care of me. Every three months, I go in for blood work to make sure the cancer hasn't recurred. The first time I had to undergo the blood tests, it was an anxious two weeks as I waited for the results. When they finally arrived and showed that the cancer was gone, I was super juiced. I went straight to the studio and made a track called "Cold Champagne for Lunch," a celebratory song about the moment I found out.

Ye the Rollie on the wrist shine
Used to walk a thin line
Now it's no more stress for months
It's cold champagne for lunch

Before my cancer diagnosis, I worked like a madman. I was chasing a number in my head: 200,000,000. I wanted a balance of two hundred million dollars, after taxes, liquid in my bank account. I don't know why I chose that exact number, but I fixated on it. I became a slave to my phone and rarely did anything for myself. Even vacations were spent taking calls, conducting business conversations, getting into arguments over plans for my companies. All work-related thoughts. That's not a life. These days, I'm trying to embrace the creativity of building a business, without the chaos. I don't need $200 million. I don't need a wildly massive exit, at the cost of my sanity, my mental and physical well-being. What I need is to enjoy what I do and continue to be great at it.

It's taken a lot to come back from litigation battles. Our public persona was dragged, but we are bouncing back. Neither the cancer nor the sharks can kill me. Beating cancer and staying relevant while being attacked by a billionaire has me feeling bulletproof.

While I always knew hyper growth would come with some hiccups, I never imagined damage to the brand like this. Thankfully the new me is here, aware of what needs to happen and ready to execute.

After five years of seeking permits, we finally have our research and development facility up and running in Humboldt County. And that's the part I'm most excited about. With the R&D lab fully operational, our dedication and focus on herb is our number one priority again after the long distraction of a legal fight. On the other side, we have interest from large investors, more control over our portfolio, and plans to IPO and build out our own production facilities in key markets across the world. When you are a visionary, you have to see it through, even when there is turbulence. It's not easy to stick to the script and stay on your path. Do it. The reward outweighs the risk.

Coming close to the possibility of death and breathing in new life forces you to put it all in perspective and really begin to care about longevity and legacy. In those early days after my surgery, when I was lying in the hospital bed thinking about what would happen if I didn't make it out of this alive, I knew I had to ensure that Cookies would be around when I'm gone. That the business would be relevant, respected, and represent everything I stood for. I began to map out a hundred-year-old brand, and that's my mission right now. The money part becomes irrelevant. Because when our time comes, all that really matters is the future we leave our children and what impact you made during your time here on earth. I'd like to live forever through my work.

My biggest fear is seeing a bunch of blue buildings around the world with no love or clear direction. Take a look at McDonald's. I'm sure many of the employees there take their jobs seriously and do good work. But at this point the business is more of a real estate play than anything, and the business doesn't represent what the founders, who were focused on the food and the service, had set out to do. So it's no surprise when there's no true morale around the brand and its purpose, and their people clock in, sell the same mass-produced crap they've been selling for years, and clock out. What is the employee supposed to be excited about? Where's the passion or motivation supposed to come from?

Lawsuits are so draining and such a buzzkill. Litigation, and everything that comes with it, began to feel like my cancer battle the longer it drew on. It's physically and mentally challenging, but I know for sure on the other side is a fresh new life for my company. That's what keeps me fighting. Anything monetary is a big fucking cherry on top.

You can be your own worst enemy in life. Being in a great headspace or looking at things from a different perspective can be a huge advantage, especially for a businessperson and entrepreneur. I used to put *so much* pressure on myself. I focused on what I thought I needed or whatever I didn't have. No more. This second shot at life is priceless.

. . .

It's such a trip. By the time you are reading this, my hope is that my company will be on its way to being listed on the NASDAQ. We'll have jumped over every major hurdle put in front of us and built Cookies into a billion-dollar brand against all odds. I've been reading the last few lines over and over again. In reality, I don't know what will happen. All of it can go a totally different way, for all I know. But looking through this new lens has taught me to manifest and truly speak—or in this case, write—things into existence. Going from a misfit kid in the Bay to a wide-eyed dreamer at the Hemp Center to a brand-builder and ambassador, I guess I've been doing it my entire career.

I said it near the beginning of this book, but for those of you that may have had a few too many joints, I'll repeat it: Life as an entrepreneur is a fucked-up roller-coaster ride. There are ups, and there are downs. And it's all about whether or not you're able to shine when you're down. During my brokest times, I remember walking into a room full of rappers with big diamond chains and $300,000 cars in the parking lot, and I knew that with the little baggie in my pocket I had something they had zero access to. Knowing that made me light the room up every single time.

Parker asked me when we started this journey, "Do you want to be the biggest? Or do you want to be the best?" My answer was, "Both." But it turns out it wasn't possible to do both at the same time. To be the best you would need to be vertically integrated and control every aspect of the supply chain to ensure quality, and that takes time and lots of capital. While that is happening, you could be missing out on opportunities or important markets as they open up. But if you first focus on being the biggest and expanding rapidly, then you can plant your flag, grab market share and global recognition, increase your value, and raise money in a far more non-dilutive way. Once you've achieved that, *then* you can go back and dial everything in the way you want to. Which is exactly what we did. It was risky, and following that road map we took plenty of hits on the chin, but look at where we are now. I'm forever grateful to be able to be in this position to look back and explain the genius of our approach and to have a chance to thank the people that stuck with us through it all.

I truly hope that, through my story and my outlook on brand-building, you were able to soak up some game and feel motivated to go get yours. Never let anyone put you in a box, and expand your wings every chance you get. Much of what you read in this book started out as a dream. All I did was see it through.

The biggest lesson I have learned through it all is that no matter how hard life gets, never quit. You will be surprised what's waiting for you on the other side. Whether it be music, clothing, cannabis, rolling papers, or film and media, each one of my companies complements the others and was built from the ground up. We have created our own little world, and I am beyond grateful that, by reading this book, you are now a part of it.

To all my entrepreneurs out there, I'll leave you with this: Being a whale isn't just about being the biggest in the sea (although that's definitely a part of it). It's about being a big fucking ball of positive energy in a sea of negativity. A whale is a business mogul who doesn't have to be seedy, like all the sharks out there circling in the water, looking to get a bite even if they have to chomp off someone's arm or leg to do it. I've always kept my head down and stayed true to myself. I never played nobody. I never lied to nobody. I've taken the high road every single time. A whale is somebody who can do big business but be honest, loved, and respected. You don't need to steal from anyone, lie to anyone, or do anything shady to win in business. So be sharp, and always stay true to your heart.

A vibrant brand needs its people to be engaged and geeked about what they're selling—it's especially true in the cannabis industry, which is driven by new flavors and hype. There is no way I can let the vision stop when I'm gone.

So here's my plan.

It's 2095. You're an employee at Cookies. You show up for your shift, and your manager gathers the team together. They tell you and your fellow co-workers to take a seat, and you notice the row of empty chairs in a semicircle. You sit down, and the manager turns down the lights. A hologram of me pops up from the center of the semicircle. It might be outdated technology by then, like if you wheeled in a TV and popped a VHS tape into a VCR today, but it'll still be dope to see me there addressing the room.

First, I show you all a plant and explain what it is and its lineage. Next comes the dry, harvested flower. As I begin to explain its unique aroma, your manager passes around turkey bags filled with that same bud. You dive your nose into it and take a big whiff and touch and examine it closely. While you're familiarizing yourself with the product, I describe the cross and the genetics and whatever else about the terps, the DNA, the smoke, the high that I personally enjoy.

I explain that I'm currently speaking to them from the year 2025 and that the genetics from the bud they are holding has been in cold storage to be saved so it could be released to the world at this precise moment in time, in 2095. I pull out a joint of the bud and spark it up. As I light my joint, your manager gives you a joint of your own to light and taste. The weed is amazing. I wrap things up with a motivational speech, talk about the good we can do in the world with this shit, and then boom, now it's on you to introduce this new menu item to our customers. Now, call me crazy, but if you saw and experienced all that, wouldn't you be excited to show it off, talk about it, and sell it? That's where my head is at right now. My main focus is genetics and brand preservation. I'm essentially planning on putting new and powerful cannabis genetics in a time machine. The way technology is developing so quickly, especially with major advancements in areas like tissue culture, it all seems possible.

The work we're undergoing there now will sustain the brand long after I am gone. We're breeding, pheno-hunting, test-running, selecting, and curating strains for the new menus we'll be releasing for the next hundred years. All of it in-house, with me still selecting the names and approving the bud. I'm setting a schedule for when each strain will be released, and I'm filming the videos that will appear in the holograms. I am dead serious about this.

Most people have a near-death experience and start thinking about where their property will go, or who they should have removed from their will. Well, I'm adding people, like my good friend Farid, who is head of content at Cookies. Farid has been working with me for over ten years and is behind most of the documentaries I've put out on my YouTube channel. He understands that Cookies is a big company and not everyone may be aware of my vision, so he's an important proxy for me when I'm not around. Point is, I'm trying to do anything I can to make sure my touch stays alive no matter what. It would break my heart to see our shit ever look cheesy or get watered down.

I refuse to let the culture die or to lose sight of the most important thing Cookies brings to the table, which is great-tasting, incredible weed and a platform to unite and bring people together. The people suing us and trying to take the brand don't share that passion. They wouldn't know what to do with the company if they got it, and that's why I'm fighting so hard to make sure the next chapter of Cookies is written on my terms.

The fact is, Cookies isn't theirs. And it isn't mine, either. It's all of ours.

We—myself, you all, talented breeders like Jai, incredible legacy cultivators, innovative thinkers like Parker, the global community of fans and smokers—we all built this shit. Together, we set trends around the world and completely changed the present and future of the cannabis industry forever. We are the world's first cannabis brand, and I am both proud and confident in saying that we paved the way for all the other brands out there today. Lately I find myself thinking about the Ron Livingston character in the movie *Office Space,* a disgruntled corporate pencil pusher who, tired of the hamster wheel, sees a hypnotist who gets him to stop worrying about everything and encourages him to do whatever he wanted to do in life. That's me these days. Free of worry and empowered to do what brings me calm and happiness. I'm in a great zone.

I used to define success as a number. That $200 million. But I'm over that binary way of thinking. My new definition of success is being able to work with who I want when I want—not any dollar amount. I've learned plenty of times that when you're having fun, the money comes. I just want to make everything with Cookies fun again. The creative compound has been electric with ideas lately. Besides mapping out the next hundred years of our brand and our menus, I've got a number of concepts in the works. One of them has to do with the apparel and accessories side of my business. I'm building a set in the compound for a show we're going to call *The Platform,* where creators and inventors will pitch me new products in person. If I like what I see, I'll work out a deal on camera right then and there for their innovation to become a Cookies product.

In exchange, the inventor will get a royalty or a potential distribution deal or an investment with one of a rotating cast of guest hosts. Your typical product engineers, dudes running up an hourly rate to bring subpar products to life, get burned out and lack the drive that leads to true innovation. I want to empower entrepreneurs and provide a platform to showcase the best, coolest new stuff out there.

This is just a small piece of my story, and being able to write this has been extremely therapeutic and has even motivated me to keep following my wild dreams. I hope it's done the same for you. Love you guys. Thank you for letting me be me.

Afterword

Parker Berling, President of Cookies

Berner and I are the same age. We both grew up in the Bay Area. We both love cannabis. But even though we grew up in the same city and we share a passion for cannabis, our paths couldn't have been more different.

I went to school at UC San Diego, where I played basketball. After graduating, I had a short stint in a financial position with a company in San Diego but left to do some traveling. I rode my bike from the northern tip of Alaska to the southern tip of Argentina. The whole journey took me two years. When I finished the trek in 2011, I returned to the Bay Area in my early twenties and got into the tech industry with a job at a marketing platform company. I started in an entry-level sales position and worked my way up and built a relationship with the CEO and president of that company, who took it public and sold it to Oracle, where I continued to work for a little while. That president went on to start a new company, a tech sales platform called Heighten, and I was fortunate enough to be brought in from the beginning. Within a few years that company was sold to LinkedIn/Microsoft, and the CEO and president went on to help take Docusign public. But I didn't join for that journey. I felt I'd missed a window of excitement in the tech world, missed what entrepreneurs had experienced during Tech 1.0 in the mid-late '90s, when they were at the starting gate during what must have been an invigorating time in an emerging industry. I made the decision to move away from tech and into cannabis.

At the time, I already owned a farm up in Humboldt County and was in the process of purchasing a five-acre commercial property called One Log right at the entrance of Humboldt (today it is Cookies' R&D facility). Humboldt is unique in that it has the climate and environment that allows you to grow extremely high-quality product outdoors or in greenhouses. Humboldt was one of the first counties to opt into the legalized program, which to this day not every county has. This was around late 2016, when the laws in California were changing to allow the first compliant sale of medical cannabis. Even though Prop 216 had been around since 1996, it was still very much a gray market in California. At that time, something like 90 percent of the cannabis sold in the United States came out of the Emerald Triangle, which consists of Humboldt, Trinity, and Mendocino counties. Growing up in that environment, selling small amounts of weed in high school and college, buying a cannabis farm as a hobby, you could say I was pretty hooked on the industry itself, and the notion of turning it into a career was really interesting to me. So I pursued the opportunity to be on the ground floor of an emerging industry that I happened to be extremely passionate about.

After the sale of Heighten, I took a more active role on the farm in Humboldt and saw a way into the industry as both an operator and an investor. Along with a few friends, some of whom are still active members of the Cookies team today, we started a cannabis venture capital firm called Mesh Ventures. Through One Log, I was getting a master's education in the industry and the various cannabis licenses, which gave me a strong sense of what we needed to target and invest in with Mesh.

That's when we set our sights on Berner and Cookies.

I don't know how you could live in the Bay Area and be a fan of cannabis and cannabis culture and *not* know exactly who Berner is. I knew his music, I knew about his streetwear and accessories business, and I knew about projects like his documentary series, *Marijuana Mania*.

Cookies was on everyone's radar in the early days of legal cannabis. Even before legalization, Cookies was probably the only brand that had international recognition. When I looked at Cookies, I saw a brand that, if we could put some real corporate infrastructure around it (in a similar way that Berner had already done with his clothing and accessories), then we could essentially just throw gasoline on the brand and ensure that Cookies maintained its position as the most recognized global brand in the cannabis space.

At Mesh, we believed that, in any consumer packaged goods (CPG) industry, the *brands* will be the winners once everything else gets commoditized. So we wanted to invest in what we thought would be the first winning brand of the cannabis industry, and we felt pretty strongly that, at least initially, the winning brands would come out of California. There were certainly a handful of brands on our radar, but to me Cookies was always the holy grail.

The power of a strong brand is the same no matter the product. Whether it be alcohol or tobacco or beverages, I can't tell you the name of any of the manufacturers, but we all know the brand on the label. Put it this way: I'm sure it's great to own a Coca-Cola bottling facility. But what you *really* want to be is Coca-Cola.

We just applied common sense and logic to an emerging CPG industry—cannabis—and approached it like you would any similar, parallel CPG industry where, of course, the brands would be the winners.

You have to understand that Berner was the very first guy to brand weed. Of course there are other strains that everybody knew at the time, but nobody had been willing to put their actual face behind it and to build a logo and a colorway around it. It was an insane risk not just to put his name behind Girl Scout Cookies, this strain that caught fire all over the world, but also to build on that to create a real brand. He was brilliant to focus first on the clothing and accessories because he could do so legally, and he found a way to protect and trademark things like the Cookies name and logo. So for us it was a no-brainer. Berner and Cookies was our number one priority; any other company would be a distant second.

I first met Berner in late 2017. We were introduced by a common friend who had heard that one of the members of our fund was building what, at that time, was one of the largest cultivation facilities, out in Oakland. Knowing what I know now, I can see that at that time Berner was looking for a group like ours that could help him turn the cannabis side of the Cookies brand into a proper company, which, given the lack of rules and regulation before legalization, had been extremely difficult. That led to us meeting at that indoor cultivation operation in Oakland.

You can think what you want about Berner, and he is a rapper with a certain image, but almost immediately I saw that he wears his heart on his sleeve in terms of the image he portrays of himself on social media as a family man and someone who is obsessed with cannabis. That's exactly who he is. But I was pleasantly surprised in terms of his business acumen and how driven he was. He's probably the hardest-working person I've ever met. The guy doesn't drink, he doesn't do drugs (other than smoke a lot of weed), but he's so incredibly laser-focused on two things: his business and his family.

From that first meeting in Oakland, I was very direct in that our goal was to invest in Cookies and help build a team around Berner. He said that's exactly what he was looking for. I explained to him who I was, my background in tech businesses and the passion and familiarity I had with the cannabis industry. Our goal, I explained, was not just to invest in the standout brands coming out of California but to help them grow. If you looked at mainstream culture at that time, Cookies was still very much a cult following; maybe one or two people out of ten knew what it was. Our goal was to get that up to like eight out of ten people. That was the genesis. With Berner and Cookies, we could take a cultural phenomenon that had built a small but loyal following and turn it into a hundred-year brand. It's a concept that Berner and I constantly talk about to this day.

We moved quickly and provided Berner and his co-founder, Jai, with a proposal to invest. That kicked off due diligence on both sides; there was excitement over a potential deal. We got down to the one-yard line on that initial investment—and unfortunately it fell through. Berner really wanted to work with us, but his partner, Jai, had been exploring another deal. They ended up moving forward with that deal, and we were devastated. The deal they took ended up trading a portion of the company for some assets that the other partner had, like farms and distribution licenses.

Luckily, by that point Berner and I had created a solid relationship. I was dead set on working with him one way or another, and I now know that Berner felt the same. So we pivoted and focused on another early-stage brand he had built, Lemonnade, which I described to everyone as the Sprite to Cookies' Coca-Cola (which was obviously Cookies). He had a logo and a group of interesting genetics, which was appealing, but really we were interested in making an investment in Berner, and Lemonnade was our foot in the door. So we made the investment in Lemonnade and began to initiate the same plans we had for Cookies with Lemonnade. And because Berner was attached to the brand, we believed that it might regain us the right to get back into the conversation with Cookies. Which is how it played out.

With Lemonnade, we launched the asset-light, capital-efficient model, which ultimately became the model we applied to Cookies. Very quickly we started to build up a team around Lemonnade, construct the family of genetics, and secure the first licensing deals for the brand. Lemonnade had agreements where it would be produced in two or three states, which is something Cookies didn't yet have. The original deal Jai and Berner went with had gotten their attention in part because of the value it could bring to them in California, but watching Lemonnade launch, they realized early on that the asset-light model would allow us to expand the brand far beyond California. California is the biggest and in many ways the most important cannabis market in the world, but I really wanted to solidify the brand in as many states and countries as possible without having to raise billions of dollars.

A lot of companies would love to pursue an asset-light, capital-efficient business model, but the thing that allows you to pull it off is the brand. That's why we were in a unique position to adopt the strategy that we did. You can list any number of the big multistate operators, but none of them had brand recognition. They were big companies with tons of capital, and they specialized in winning licenses to set up supply chains in various markets. But if you're a company with no brand, then you have no choice. That is the only path you have. Nobody is going to build the infrastructure for you, because there's no incentive to do so. We saw these other companies raising hundreds of millions, which soon became billions, of dollars and building really expensive infrastructure all over the world—the United States, Canada, Europe. And Cookies was behind the ball in that.

By April 2019, Cookies came back to the table, as we had hoped, and we finally made our investment. By that point, a lot of other companies in the space had already been spending years building their own supply chains. They had a massive head start in terms of capital raising. So we had two options: Go down the same path and beat the other guys at their own game of raising a tremendous amount of cash and building our own infrastructure. Or leverage the one thing we had that they didn't: the brand.

Now, instead of building these huge facilities all around the world, we would adopt the logical strategy of finding who we felt were the best operators and cultivators in each market and licensing our brand to those operators. The next logical step after that would be to do something similar on the retail side: Find folks who had won the best licenses but didn't want to open their own retail brand, or find existing stores that were up and operating where the principal owners believed that they could significantly increase revenue by converting their storefronts into Cookies stores.

We knew there would be pros and cons to that model.

The pros: With a low barrier to entry, this will help us gain brand recognition around the world. That was the primary goal.

The cons: If you don't own and control your supply chain, there are challenges in terms of quality and consistency.

Owning your own supply chain is very nice, but it takes a really long time and it's really expensive. Instead, we said, "Let's blow the brand up, and then at some point we'll flip the script and look into owning and operating our own facilities." Which is the chapter of Cookies that we are embarking on now.

I knew and had realized by that time that I really loved operating. And I wanted to put my shoulder behind Cookies, which was easily our biggest investment. The way I saw it, it meant the difference between coaching and playing. I wanted to be on the court and have a more direct role in determining the success of the team. The investor position was more akin to the coaching role; I wanted the ball in my hands. There was no company that I wanted to do that more with than Cookies and no partner I wanted to share the court with more than Berner.

After investing the rest of our capital into Cookies, Mesh Ventures closed its fund. I was playing a very active role in Cookies already, but as an investor. As part of Mesh's investment, Mesh got a board seat, and I held that seat. But very soon after, Berner, myself, and the other investors agreed that I would formally take over management and become the president of the company.

Our model was allowing the Cookies brand to gain significant ground, but we had to adjust our vision as we went along. For example, we never really intended to be a retail company at all. But after the opportunity to open our first Cookies store in Maywood, California, came about, it blew our minds. In the very first month after opening the doors we did a million dollars in that single location. We all looked at each other and said, "Well, I guess we're a retail company now, too." It just felt like a no-brainer to continue down that path. We were determined to use the brand to the full extent of its powers.

As Cookies has grown to what *Business Insider* called "America's first $1 billion weed brand," the same dynamic exists between Berner and me as when we first began working together. Berner is the best I've ever seen in terms of not just understanding trends but setting them. My first company sold marketing software to Fortune 500 companies, and I worked with a lot of CMOs of some of the biggest retailers in the world, and I would put Berner right up there against any one of them in terms of their ability to understand the industry that they were marketing in. From day one, we had an understanding that the marketing side of the business—creatives, design, product development, and selection—is 100 percent Berner's world. I would never want to encroach on that, and I wanted his vision to be protected. We could never compromise his vision with the side of the business that I focused on, which was building the corporate infrastructure around Berner and Cookies.

But that doesn't mean we haven't encountered significant hurdles. The drama surrounding one of our biggest investors, SI, is a major example. And it was extremely difficult to navigate. SI was one of the closest things to institutional capital in the industry. I knew who the principals were because they also had a multibillion-dollar fund, which was more of a typical Silicon Valley venture capital group. They were major, major players. The value they offered early on and pitched us on was that they were going to be one of the leading investors in the cannabis space and the only investors we would need going forward. The billionaire behind the fund was going to be Berner's mentor, and they would help me with building the business. It was really attractive for us. Plus, as Berner put it, he didn't want to just have all his eggs in one basket with Mesh. So it made sense to get involved with SI on a number of levels. We expected to get a lot of value out of the partnership. But you learn in business that sometimes things don't go as planned.

I don't think I yet appreciated how incredibly important it is to know who you are taking money from. There's a lot of private equity disguised as venture. A lot of groups saying, "We want to invest with a venture mindset. We're looking for big returns and long hold periods." And I think unfortunately what a lot of people learn is that many of those seemingly venture-focused investment firms quickly become predatory private equity and want to take control of the company that they have invested in. That is certainly what happened with us, and I don't think we were unique in that learning. Unfortunately, there are a lot of brands out there that didn't have the Cookies name, and many have gone under because of the pressure that has been put on them by these predatory investors.

Another major hurdle has been the litigation we've been dragged through. It's debilitating. Courts have ruled in our favor to the tune of nearly $20 million in awards, and it is vindicating, in a sense, in the face of the horrible things our investors at SI said about us that were complete lies. But make no mistake: There is no ruling that we could get that I would choose over never having to be in this position in the first place. Being in litigation like this puts your company in purgatory. It stalled us out in terms of what we were trying to do.

The goal has always been to get to this point of leveraging the asset-light model to the point that we have achieved phase one, which is international brand recognition and solidifying Cookies as the biggest brand in cannabis. We got recognized by *Ad Age* as Brand of the Year—the first cannabis brand to get that award. And then when Berner got on the cover of *Forbes,* at that point we looked at each other and said, "I think it's time for phase two." Phase two is the transition away from the asset-light model to strategically build our supply chain and gain more control of our actual operations. The litigation has made that second phase incredibly difficult. It's made it really hard to do just about anything, to be honest. The overhang of that kind of litigation is a lot to overcome, but I think we've done an incredible job in growing and keeping the brand relevant. But the opportunity cost that we've lost from this makes you want to cry.

That said, we are weathering the storm. Our strategy hasn't

changed; it's just the pace at which we can execute that second phase has slowed. We've had to extend our timelines as a result. On top of that, the events in the cannabis industry beyond our control aren't making anything easier. The name of the game right now really is: survive. Everyone is just waiting for federal regulations to change. Whether that's full legalization, or rescheduling, or even safe banking—one of those three things is going to be the catalyst that all of us are waiting for, which will launch Cannabis 2.0.

I see a lot of parallels between tech and cannabis. In Tech 1.0 you had the vaporware companies that didn't really make any money, didn't have much of a platform, and yet had multibillion-dollar valuations. And coming out of that phase a bunch of bullshit companies went under. And that led to Tech 2.0, where you had real companies, like Alphabet or Nvidia, that made those frothy valuations of Tech 1.0 look like child's play.

Looking back, I didn't anticipate the time horizon in cannabis. Even in 2019, when I joined Cookies, we felt we were on the precipice of federal legalization. We did a pretty good job of not putting too many eggs in that basket, but there's no question it impacted the way everyone was running their companies. For us, we'd utilized this asset-light model and built a big portfolio of assets that we had purchase options on. Our goal was—is—to execute on those options in conjunction with a U.S. IPO. Nobody at that time would have believed that by 2025 there had been no progress on that front.

We're sitting and waiting for that catalyst to help us reach that next phase for the cannabis industry. Because right now it's impossible for everyone to grow. There is no institutional capital, and most of the family office and high net-worth individuals who invested in Cannabis 1.0 got burned. So the only capital available to this industry has dried up, and it will remain dry until we see some sort of change that will allow this fresh batch of capital to come in. Everyone is trying to survive and waiting, and unfortunately, you're seeing a ton of brands and companies disappear. With the power of our brand and the vision and dedication of our team, Cookies won't be one of them.

Acknowledgments

A lot of the stories, moments, and memories in this book are super personal, and I've never shared them with anyone. I've been waiting for this opportunity to share them all with my day-ones, and I'm so proud to do it on a platform like this. I've kept my mouth shut for years and held off on speaking too much on podcasts and interviews. Thank you for always letting me be an open book with all of you. Some of this stuff is not easy for me to speak about, and was hard to hold in, but it was so worth the wait.

I wouldn't be who I am or where I'm at today if it weren't for the people around me. To my beautiful family: You are the balance to this wild journey, the motivation to keep going and fight for what we've built. Janelle, you gave me hope and vision in dark times. You made me elevate and showed me what life was really about. I'm forever thankful for the bond and connection we have, and watching you become a woman has been one of the best parts of my life. Thank you. I'm beyond thankful for my wife, Ashley. What a fairy-tale situation we have—the definition of true love. Every businessman needs a strong woman. I'm glad I found you. I'm excited to grow old with you, babe. Thank you for sticking with me during the roller-coaster ride.

To my son, Gilbert: I get goosebumps when I picture your smile. I've always wanted a son but never imagined how incredibly perfect you would be. You have that light when you enter the room. People are addicted to you within seconds. Your energy is powerful—never forget that. To my daughter Jodi: From the moment you arrived, I could feel how special and beautiful your soul is. I enjoy our conversations in the mornings (in baby talk, of course) and I cannot wait to take you and your brother to Hawaii this Christmas. Daddy loves you.

I want to take some time to shine light on my supporters. Take a step back and look at what we built. Wow. We did this. We built a hundred-year brand from the mud and did it in the most organic way possible. Thank you. And thank you for letting me be me. I've never had to put on an act or be in character for you—you accepted the real me and that's the biggest blessing. Set aside the music career, the clothing brand, and Cookies' cannabis arm . . . You helped me beat cancer. I was open and public about that battle, and I truly believe I wouldn't be here without you guys. I love you for that.

Erick, Charles & Chris: Thank you guys so much. We launched this monster from my living room and took it to the moon. I want to thank all my partners at Cookies—Jai, Bill, and the warehouse; and all our cultivation partners, retail operators, brand partners, and breeders; and, of course, all our employees. We have been through hell and back and I appreciate you staying along for the ride. We built something that nobody could ever take away from us. We planted our flag and made fucking history. Thank you, Ian and Crystal. You both work your asses off!

Parker: Thank you, brother. Thank you for the loyalty, love, and insane dedication to seeing this through. We've had such a painful three years fighting for our baby. Being an entrepreneur is not easy and staring at the wall at four in the morning definitely hurts sometimes. Knowing that you have love and respect for this brand makes it possible. You're the perfect example of a partner and one of the most important mentors of mine. Appreciate you, bro, I really do.

To my father: Thank you for coming into my life the way you

did when I lost my mother. I really needed you and I love you. My brother Matt: Keep outworking me. You're building something special. To my sister, Mellissa, and brother Geoff, I love you so much. Vinny and Sassy, you two have been such good siblings to Janelle. I'm so glad to have been able to be a part of your lives and help raise you to be such beautiful people. I love you guys.

I also want to give a huge shout-out to Genesee, Cozmo, Traxx FDR, Max Pery, Stinje, and Drew for helping to find and develop my sound on the music side of things. We've made some real classics.

And last but not least, I've got to show some love and thank the GAME and the legacy industry. Remember to stay strong and never let anyone devalue what you bring to the table. We risked our freedom for this shit. Don't give up!

About the Author

BERNER, born Gilbert Anthony Milam, Jr., is the co-founder and CEO of Cookies, the most globally recognized cannabis brand in the world. He is also a *Billboard*-charting hip-hop artist. He is the first cannabis CEO to both grace the cover of *Forbes* magazine and have a *New York Times* profile. He lives in the Bay Area, California.

Instagram: @berner415

About the Type

This book was set in Sabon, a typeface designed by the well-known German typographer Jan Tschichold (1902–74). Sabon's design is based upon the original letter forms of sixteenth-century French type designer Claude Garamond and was created specifically to be used for three sources: foundry type for hand composition, Linotype, and Monotype. Tschichold named his typeface for the famous Frankfurt typefounder Jacques Sabon (c. 1520–80).